Retire Without a Pension

Plan and Invest with 401k, IRA, and Social Security

Matthew Thomas

A Note before You Start

Nothing in this book is professional financial, tax, or legal advice. The numbers and strategies here are meant to show you how the pieces fit together, not to tell you exactly what to do with your money.

Tax laws change. Social Security rules shift. Medicare costs and ACA subsidy structures get adjusted by Congress on schedules few people can predict. What's accurate in 2026 may not apply in 2031. Before making major decisions — claiming Social Security, converting retirement accounts, buying insurance — talk to someone who knows your full picture.

We've tried to be honest about trade-offs and uncertainty throughout. The places where things get complicated are where simplifying would have been dishonest. Trust professionals who know your situation over any general guidance, including this.

Acknowledgments

Thanks to everyone who talked openly about the gap between what standard retirement advice promises and what it delivers — the people who ran the numbers at 50 and didn't like what they saw, who got blindsided by ACA premiums or Medicare costs or the realization that the math just didn't work.

Those conversations shaped this book more than any research did.

The Untold Numbers

Karen had worked for the same hospital system for 31 years. She was a radiology technician, good at her job, careful with money by the standards of her life — she'd paid off the house, put two kids through state schools, never carried credit card debt past the end of the month. She had a 403b. She contributed enough to get the match, most years a little more. At 58, she started thinking seriously about retiring at 62.

She went online and read that she needed a million dollars. She had $380,000 in her 403b and the house, which was worth maybe $210,000 after years of paying it down. She was nowhere close.

Then she read that she needed 80% of her pre-retirement income. She was making $67,000. Eighty percent was $53,600. That sounded like a lot. She went back to worrying.

What Karen didn't know — couldn't know, because few people had laid it out for her — was that the million-dollar rule and the 80% rule were both built for somebody else's life. She was already spending about $44,000 per year: mortgage paid, kids out of the house, no commute costs she'd have in retirement because she'd be home. With Social Security of $1,640 a month if she waited until 67, that was $19,680 per year. The gap between what she spent and what Social Security would provide was $24,320. At a 4% withdrawal rate, covering that gap required $608,000, not a million.

She wasn't as far behind as she thought. She also wasn't as close as she wanted to be. But the real number — the one that mattered for her life — was very different from the number she'd been handed.

This book is about finding that real number and building toward it with the tools that exist for people who don't have pensions, who work regular jobs, who made some mistakes and some good decisions and are now trying to figure out what's possible.

We need to start with the actual calculation, not the generic advice that floats around about saving a million dollars or replacing 80% of pre-retirement income. These shortcuts might work for someone, somewhere, but they completely miss the specific circumstances that determine whether we can actually retire or whether we're setting ourselves up to run out of money at 78. The number we need depends on what we're spending now, what changes when we stop working, where we plan to live, how long we might need the money to last, and how healthcare costs will compound over decades when insurance premiums and medical expenses grow faster than general inflation.

The million-dollar target gets thrown around so much that it's become meaningless, and the 80% replacement rate assumes our retirement spending will be 80% of what we earned while working, which ignores the reality that what we spend and what we earn are often very different numbers. Someone earning $100,000 who saves 15% and pays 25% in total taxes is actually living on $60,000, and replacing 80% of their income gives them $80,000 in retirement, which is more than they were spending while working. Meanwhile someone earning $60,000 who saves nothing and has minimal taxes might be spending close to $55,000, and 80% replacement gives them only $48,000, forcing lifestyle cuts they didn't anticipate.

We need to work backward from actual spending rather than forward from earnings, starting with what money goes out the door right now for housing, food, transportation, insurance, healthcare, utilities, entertainment, travel, and everything else, then adjusting for what changes when work stops. This requires looking at bank statements and credit card bills for the past year, adding up the recurring expenses and the sporadic ones, accounting for the annual insurance premiums and property taxes that don't hit every month, and facing the uncomfortable reality of how much we're actually spending rather than how much we think we're spending or wish we were spending.

Spending in retirement looks different from spending while working in ways that most people don't anticipate until they're close enough to see it clearly. The commute disappears, taking gas and car maintenance with it, and for someone driving 30 miles each way five days a week, that's 15,000 miles annually at maybe 50 cents per mile when we factor in gas, oil changes, tire wear, and the accelerated depreciation from high mileage, saving $7,500 per year. Professional clothing sits unused when we're not showing up to an office, and depending on the job this might mean $1,000-3,000 per year in suits, dresses, dry cleaning, and shoes that we no longer need to buy or maintain. Lunch money evaporates when we're not buying sandwiches near the office five days a week, potentially saving another $2,000-3,000 annually if we were eating out regularly.

The 401k contributions stop, obviously, since we're no longer earning a paycheck, and for someone contributing $23,000 per year this immediately frees up that money, though of course we were never actually spending it so this isn't a real reduction in living expenses. FICA taxes disappear once we're living on savings instead of wages, since Social Security and Medicare taxes only apply to earned income, saving 7.65% on every dollar of wages replaced by portfolio withdrawals. Someone who was earning $80,000 and paying $6,120 in FICA no longer pays this when living on IRA withdrawals, though they still pay income tax on Traditional IRA distributions just like they paid income tax on wages.

These reductions add up to something real, maybe 15-20% of what we were spending before, but they get offset partially or completely by other expenses that grow. Healthcare becomes the monster expense that pension-era retirement advice barely mentioned because employer coverage used to continue or Medicare seemed cheap enough to ignore. From age 50 to 65, we're paying full freight for insurance if we retire before Medicare eligibility, and this means anywhere from $600 to $1,500 per month per person depending on where we live, how old we are, and whether we can manage our income to qualify for ACA subsidies that reduce premiums dramatically for people showing lower income on their tax returns.

A healthy 55-year-old couple in a moderate-cost area might pay $1,200 per month for ACA coverage without subsidies, which is $14,400 per year, and this likely replaces employer coverage that was costing them maybe $300 per month in premiums deducted from paychecks, so the net increase is $10,800 annually. If they can structure their income to qualify for subsidies by keeping Modified Adjusted Gross Income under 400% of Federal Poverty

Level, around $73,240 for a couple in 2024, their premiums might drop to $400-600 per month total, making the increase more like $2,400-4,800 over what they were paying with employer coverage.

After 65, Medicare looks cheaper at first glance because Part B premiums start at $174.70 per month in 2024, and Part D for prescriptions might add another $40-60 per month, and Medigap coverage to fill the gaps runs $150-300 per month depending on age and location, bringing total monthly costs to maybe $400-600 per person. For a couple this means $800-1,200 per month or $9,600-14,400 annually, which might be less than they were paying on the ACA marketplace but is certainly more than employer coverage was costing, and this is before we pay anything out of pocket for actual care.

The out-of-pocket costs grow as we age because Medicare doesn't cover everything and our bodies need more maintenance in our 70s and 80s than they did in our 50s and 60s. Copays for doctor visits, prescription medications, dental work, vision care, hearing aids, and all the other things that Medicare doesn't fully cover can easily run $3,000-5,000 per year for a healthy couple, and someone with chronic conditions might spend $8,000-12,000 annually even with good supplemental coverage. By our 80s, medical expenses excluding insurance premiums can hit $10,000-15,000 per year for a couple as prescription costs increase, specialist visits multiply, and the wear and tear of aging bodies requires more intervention.

Long-term care sits out there as a potential six-figure cost that most people either ignore or handle through spending down to Medicaid qualification. Nursing home care runs about $105,000 per year nationally in 2024, with significant variation by location from maybe $75,000 in lower-cost states to $150,000 in expensive cities, and assisted living costs less at around $60,000 per year but still represents a massive expense if needed for several years. The average nursing home stay lasts 2-3 years, though some people need care for much longer, and at $105,000 per year this means $210,000-315,000 in costs that Medicare doesn't cover beyond the first 100 days after hospitalization.

We can buy long-term care insurance to transfer this risk, paying $2,000-5,000 per year in premiums for coverage that might pay $150-200 per day for 3-5 years, or we can self-insure by building enough assets to cover the potential costs ourselves, or we can plan to spend down to Medicaid qualification if the need arises, accepting the limited choice of facilities and care options that Medicaid provides. Each approach has trade-offs, and someone with $2 million saved might reasonably self-insure by planning to use $400,000 for long-term care if needed, while someone with $800,000 total can't afford to dedicate half the portfolio to a potential expense and might need insurance or Medicaid planning.

Travel and discretionary spending might increase in early retirement when we're healthy and have time, then decrease as we age and slow down, creating a spending pattern that's higher from 60-75 and lower from 75 onward. The conventional wisdom that spending declines in retirement ignores the reality that many people spend more in the first decade after retiring because they're finally doing the traveling and hobbies they postponed while working, then spend less in their late 70s and 80s when mobility decreases and interests shift toward staying home. Someone planning to spend $50,000 per year in retirement might actually need $60,000 from 60-70, $50,000 from 70-80, and $45,000 from 80 onward, excluding healthcare which increases throughout.

Inflation over 30 or 40 years does more damage than we typically imagine when we're planning in today's dollars, because 3% annual inflation doesn't sound threatening but it cuts purchasing power in half over 24 years and by two-thirds over 37 years. Something costing $40,000 this year costs $54,000 in 10 years at 3% inflation, $72,000 in 20 years, $97,000 in 30 years, and $131,000 in 40 years. We need to think about buying power across decades, not just the initial withdrawal amount, because the person retiring at 55 and living to 95 is funding four decades of price increases on everything from groceries to property taxes to insurance premiums.

Healthcare inflation runs even higher than general inflation, historically averaging 5-7% annually, which means medical expenses double every 10-14 years instead of every 24 years like general expenses. Someone spending

$15,000 per year on healthcare at age 65 might be spending $30,000 at 75, $60,000 at 85, and $120,000 at 95 if healthcare inflation continues at 7%, though in practice we hope to die before expenses get that extreme or we've long since exhausted our assets and landed on Medicaid. Even at 5% healthcare inflation, which is optimistic, that $15,000 at 65 becomes $24,000 at 75 and $39,000 at 85, representing an increasing share of total spending as we age.

The mathematical relationship between inflation and required portfolio size is non-linear because we need the portfolio to generate increasing amounts each year to maintain purchasing power, which means we're withdrawing both the initial amount and the cumulative inflation adjustments. Starting with $40,000 in year one, we need $41,200 in year two at 3% inflation, $42,436 in year three, $43,709 in year four, and by year 30 we need $97,000 to buy what $40,000 bought initially. The 4% rule accounts for this by adjusting the withdrawal upward each year, but the portfolio needs to grow enough to support these increasing withdrawals while also sustaining the periodic market downturns that reduce its value.

Geographic variation matters more than most retirement calculators acknowledge because cost of living differences compound over decades into hundreds of thousands of dollars in different required savings. Living in San Francisco on $70,000 per year feels completely different from living in Pensacola on the same amount, and the difference isn't just lifestyle preference but actual survival math that determines whether retirement is feasible with the assets we've accumulated. Housing alone creates massive variation, with median rents running $3,500 per month in expensive cities versus $1,500 in cheaper areas, a difference of $24,000 annually that persists year after year.

Property taxes vary wildly by location even for similar-valued homes, with some states charging 0.5% of home value annually while others charge 2% or more, and on a $400,000 home this means the difference between $2,000 and $8,000 per year. State income taxes range from 0% in Florida, Texas, and several other states to 13.3% in California for high earners, and someone withdrawing $60,000 per year from Traditional IRA might pay nothing in state tax in Florida versus $3,000-5,000 in California depending on their total income and deductions. Sales taxes, car registration fees, utility costs, and insurance premiums all vary by state and city, creating aggregate cost differences that can easily reach $20,000-30,000 annually between expensive and cheap locations.

Someone with $800,000 saved might struggle to retire in Boston or San Francisco but live comfortably in Albuquerque or Pensacola, and this isn't about being frugal versus extravagant but about structural cost differences that compound over decades. If we need $70,000 per year to maintain our desired lifestyle in an expensive city, and Social Security provides $30,000, we must generate $40,000 from our portfolio, which at 4% withdrawal rate requires $1 million. If we can live on $45,000 per year in a cheaper location with the same $30,000 Social Security, we need only $15,000 from the portfolio, requiring $375,000 in savings, a difference of $625,000 that might represent 10-15 years of additional working or the difference between retirement being possible or impossible.

The calculation starts with current spending minus what drops off plus what increases, adjusted for inflation over the expected retirement length, modified by geographic location, and then we work backward to figure out the portfolio size needed to generate that spending when combined with Social Security. For someone needing $50,000 per year in today's dollars who expects Social Security to provide $24,000, we're looking at $26,000 that must come from savings, which at a 4% withdrawal rate requires $650,000, but that's the starting point before we account for healthcare cost increases above general inflation, the possibility of needing long-term care, and the risk of living longer than average.

The 4% rule suggests we can withdraw 4% of our starting portfolio balance in year one, then increase that dollar amount by inflation each year, and have a 95% probability of the money lasting 30 years based on historical market returns and inflation rates. This means starting with $650,000 and withdrawing $26,000 in year one, $26,780 in year two if inflation is 3%, and continuing to adjust upward annually regardless of how the portfolio performs. In good years when the market is up 20%, we take out only our inflation-adjusted amount and let the excess growth accumulate. In bad years when the market is down 15%, we still take out our inflation-adjusted amount even though this requires selling more shares at lower prices.

The 95% success rate sounds reassuring until we consider that a 5% failure rate means one in twenty people following this strategy will run out of money before they die, and if we're planning a 30-year retirement from 65 to 95, a 5% chance of complete portfolio depletion isn't nothing. The failure typically happens when we retire into a market downturn and experience poor returns in the first decade, because withdrawing money while the portfolio is declining locks in losses that never recover even when markets eventually bounce back. Someone who retired in 2007 with $1 million watched it drop to $600,000 by early 2009 even after accounting for their withdrawals, and it took many years to recover, leaving them permanently behind someone who retired in 2009 at the market bottom.

We can reduce failure risk by starting with a lower withdrawal rate, maybe 3.5% instead of 4%, which increases the required portfolio size proportionally but provides more cushion against market volatility and longer lifespans. Needing $26,000 from the portfolio at 3.5% withdrawal rate requires $743,000 instead of $650,000, an increase of $93,000 that might mean working two more years but provides much greater confidence the money will last. Alternatively we can build flexibility into spending so we can reduce withdrawals in down markets, cutting the discretionary vacation and restaurant spending when the portfolio drops below certain thresholds, then resuming higher spending when it recovers.

The honest assessment of how much we need involves several uncomfortable calculations that force us to confront whether retirement is actually feasible with our current savings trajectory. We take current age, current savings, realistic saving rate going forward, expected Social Security benefit, and desired retirement age, then run the numbers to see if the math works. Someone who is 45 years old with $150,000 saved, contributing $15,000 per year, planning to retire at 65, and expecting Social Security of $2,200 per month needs to determine if they can accumulate enough to fund the gap between their spending needs and that Social Security income.

At $15,000 per year for 20 years with 7% returns, the $150,000 grows to about $880,000 by 65, assuming no job changes that interrupt savings and no major financial emergencies that require tapping the accounts early. Social Security provides $26,400 per year, and if we need $55,000 annually to live, we must generate $28,600 from the portfolio, requiring $715,000 at 4% withdrawal rate. The $880,000 we've accumulated exceeds this by $165,000, providing some cushion for healthcare cost increases, market downturns, or living longer than expected, though not a huge cushion and certainly not enough to handle early retirement or extensive long-term care costs.

If that same person wants to retire at 60 instead of 65, they have only 15 years to save, accumulating about $600,000 instead of $880,000, and their Social Security benefit will be reduced because they have fewer years of earnings and might claim early at 62, perhaps dropping to $1,700 per month or $20,400 per year. Now they need to generate $34,600 from the portfolio, requiring $865,000, but they only have $600,000, creating a shortfall of $265,000. Early retirement is simply not possible with their current savings trajectory, and they must either increase saving rate dramatically, work longer, reduce retirement spending expectations, or accept that early retirement isn't happening.

The reverse calculation works from desired retirement spending and age to determine required savings, showing us exactly how far behind or ahead we are. Someone wanting to retire at 55 with $60,000 annual spending who expects $18,000 from Social Security needs to generate $42,000 from their portfolio, requiring $1,050,000 at 4% withdrawal rate. If they're currently 40 with $200,000 saved and contributing $20,000 per year, they can accumulate about $830,000 by 55, falling short by $220,000 and needing to either save more, work longer, or adjust spending expectations downward.

Each additional year of work accomplishes three things simultaneously that compound the impact on retirement feasibility: one more year of contributions adding to the portfolio, one more year of investment growth on the existing balance, and one fewer year the portfolio needs to fund, while also potentially increasing Social Security benefits if that additional year of earnings replaces a lower-earning year in the calculation. Working from 65 to 70 with $20,000 annual contributions and 7% returns grows an $800,000 portfolio to about $1,230,000, adding $430,000 through a combination of contributions and growth, while also reducing the retirement period from 30 years to 25 years if we expect to live to 95, and increasing Social Security benefits by perhaps 30% from delaying claim to age 70 instead of taking it at 65.

The power of working longer gets underestimated because we focus on the unpleasantness of working instead of the mathematical transformation it creates. Someone who would run out of money at 80 with early retirement at 60 might die with $500,000 unspent by retiring at 68, and the difference is eight years of contributions, growth, and reduced portfolio stress that completely changes the outcome. This doesn't make working longer emotionally appealing, but it does make it the most powerful lever available for people whose savings are insufficient for their desired retirement age.

Geographic arbitrage provides another major lever by reducing required portfolio size through lower spending rather than increasing portfolio size through more saving. Moving from San Francisco to Pensacola might cut housing costs from $3,500 to $1,500 per month, reduce property taxes from $12,000 to $2,400 per year, eliminate state income tax saving $3,000-5,000 annually, and lower general cost of living by $5,000-8,000 through cheaper groceries, utilities, car insurance, and services. Total savings of $35,000-40,000 per year translates to needing $875,000-1,000,000 less in portfolio at 4% withdrawal rate, which might represent the difference between retirement being feasible and impossible.

The hidden costs of geographic moves include the actual moving expense of $10,000-20,000 for a cross-country move, the emotional cost of leaving friends and family, the potential isolation and loneliness in a new location, reduced access to specialized healthcare and cultural amenities, and the risk that we'll need to move back if health declines and we need family support, paying moving costs twice and losing the benefit of the initial relocation. These costs are real but intangible, and each person must weigh them against the financial benefit based on their own circumstances, family situation, and willingness to adapt to a new environment.

International retirement offers even larger cost reductions but amplifies the complications and risks beyond domestic moves. Moving to Mexico, Portugal, Thailand, or Costa Rica might cut total living costs from $60,000 to $30,000 per year, creating $750,000 less required savings at 4% withdrawal rate, but this assumes stable currency exchange rates, continued access to quality healthcare, manageable visa and residency requirements, and tolerance for being far from family and U.S. support systems. Medicare doesn't work abroad except for limited border coverage, meaning we're either buying local insurance, paying out of pocket, or returning to the U.S. for major medical care, and each approach has costs and complications that reduce the nominal savings from lower cost of living.

The calculation of how much we need is simultaneously simpler and more complex than most retirement planning suggests. Simpler because it really does come down to expected spending minus Social Security equals portfolio withdrawal needs divided by safe withdrawal rate equals required portfolio size. More complex because expected spending involves projecting decades of inflation including higher healthcare inflation, geographic choices that might change over time, lifestyle adjustments we may or may not be willing to make, and the unknowable timing of our death and whether we'll need expensive long-term care near the end.

We can't know exactly how much we'll need because we can't predict market returns, inflation rates, our longevity, our healthcare costs, or whether Social Security benefits get cut before we claim them. What we can do is build scenarios around different assumptions, identify the range of likely outcomes, and save toward the higher end of that range while maintaining flexibility to adjust spending if markets perform poorly or we live longer than expected. Someone who saves $1 million instead of $800,000 has options if things go badly, including the option to spend more in early retirement when health is good, knowing there's cushion for later uncertainty.

The people who run out of money in retirement usually didn't save too little in some absolute sense but rather retired too early relative to their savings, spent too much relative to their portfolio size, failed to adjust spending when markets declined, or encountered healthcare costs that exceeded what they planned for. Someone with $600,000 who retires at 62, withdraws $35,000 annually plus inflation, lives to 92, and needs nursing home care for three years is extremely likely to deplete their portfolio, not because $600,000 is inherently insufficient but because the combination of early retirement, 30-year timeframe, moderate withdrawal rate, and long-term care costs exceeds what that portfolio can sustain.

The same person with the same $600,000 who works until 68, withdraws $28,000 annually, avoids nursing home care through in-home support or family assistance, and dies at 85 might end their life with money left over, and the difference is six additional years of work, slightly lower withdrawal rate, shorter retirement period, and avoiding the catastrophic long-term care expense. Both scenarios are realistic, and the challenge of retirement planning is that we won't know which scenario we're living until we're in it, by which point the major decisions about when to retire and how much to spend have already been made and can't be easily reversed.

This uncertainty argues for conservatism in planning, saving more than we think we need, retiring later than we might want, and maintaining spending flexibility so we can cut back if necessary. It also argues for regular reassessment every few years in retirement, checking whether the portfolio is performing as expected, whether spending is tracking to plan, whether healthcare costs are within projected ranges, and whether we need to make adjustments before small problems become unfixable. Someone who realizes at 70 that they're spending too much and the portfolio is declining can cut back and probably be fine. Someone who realizes the same thing at 82 has fewer options and less time for the portfolio to recover.

The real number we need is the amount that lets us sleep at night, knowing we've saved enough to handle normal retirement scenarios and have some cushion for the abnormal ones. For some people this might be 25 times annual spending, for others it might be 30 times or 35 times, and the difference often comes down to risk tolerance, family history of longevity, health status, and whether we have backup plans like family who could help or willingness to reduce spending significantly if needed. There's no single right answer, but there are wrong answers, and retiring with obviously insufficient assets hoping the market performs well or that we die before the money runs out is choosing to fail unless we get lucky.

The real number gives us a target. But a target with a 95% probability of lasting 30 years is very different from a target with a 75% probability. Before we can know whether our number is good enough, we need to understand what good enough means — and why some retirement plans that look identical on paper produce wildly different outcomes depending on when the bad years happen.

How Retirement Plans Fail

Monte Carlo simulation sounds technical but the concept is simple enough: run the retirement scenario thousands of times with different sequences of market returns and count how many times we run out of money before dying. The computer generates random market returns based on historical patterns, simulates withdrawing our planned amount each year adjusted for inflation, tracks how the portfolio performs through decades of ups and downs, and records whether we reach the end of our planned retirement period with money remaining or whether the portfolio hits zero while we're still alive. Running this process 10,000 times gives us a distribution of outcomes, and we can count what percentage ended with portfolio depletion to get the failure rate.

A 95% success rate means that in 500 out of 10,000 simulations, the portfolio hit zero while we were still alive, and we need to decide whether those odds feel acceptable or terrifying. If we're planning a 30-year retirement and have a 5% chance of running out of money, that's one in twenty people in our situation who will face complete portfolio depletion, needing to live on Social Security alone and whatever family support or social safety net might be available. For some people this risk is acceptable because they have family who could help, or because their Social Security benefit is large enough to cover basic needs, or because they're willing to drastically reduce spending if necessary. For others this 5% risk is unacceptable because they have no backup plan and the consequences of failure are homelessness or complete dependence on children.

The problem with success rates presented as binary pass-fail is that they reduce a continuous range of outcomes to a simple yes or no, when the actual experience of retirement involves constant adjustment based on how the portfolio is performing. Running out of money at 85 after 30 years of comfortable retirement is different from running out at 70 after 15 years, and barely scraping by with $50,000 left at death is different from dying with $800,000 unspent, but most Monte Carlo results treat all failures the same and all successes the same. This obscures important information about the severity and timing of potential failures, making it harder to assess whether a given strategy is reasonable or reckless.

We can dig deeper into the simulation results by looking at percentile outcomes rather than just success rate. The median outcome shows what happens in the middle scenario where half the simulations end with more money and half with less, telling us the most likely result if our retirement falls in the middle of the historical return distribution. The 25th percentile shows what happens in bad scenarios where three-quarters of simulations ended better and only one-quarter ended worse, giving us a sense of downside risk. The 10th percentile shows quite bad scenarios, and the 5th percentile shows the really terrible outcomes where almost everything went wrong.

Looking at these percentiles for someone retiring with $800,000, withdrawing $35,000 annually adjusted for inflation, planning a 30-year retirement, we might see median ending balance of $1,200,000, meaning half the time they ended with more than they started despite 30 years of withdrawals because market returns exceeded the withdrawal rate. The 25th percentile might show $400,000 remaining, indicating that even in moderately bad scenarios they had money left. The 10th percentile might show $80,000 remaining, meaning they cut it close but survived. The 5th percentile shows portfolio depletion around year 28, running out of money two years before the planned 30-year retirement ended.

This distribution tells us the strategy is probably reasonable because only in the worst 5% of scenarios do they actually fail, and even then they made it 28 years before depletion, but it also shows the risk isn't zero and someone experiencing poor returns early could face real hardship in their late 80s. Adjusting the strategy to reduce failure rate might involve reducing initial withdrawal to $32,000 instead of $35,000, which decreases the failure rate from 5% to perhaps 2%, or starting with $900,000 instead of $800,000 through additional saving, which provides the same improvement in success rate while maintaining the desired spending level.

Sequence of returns risk explains why two people with identical portfolios and identical average returns can end up in completely different places, because withdrawing money during the down years locks in losses that never recover while withdrawing during the up years preserves capital that can grow later. The person retiring in 2007 with a million dollars and withdrawing $40,000 per year watched their portfolio drop to $600,000 by early 2009 even accounting for their withdrawals, because the 50% market decline from peak to trough combined with continuing withdrawals meant selling shares at depressed prices. Even after the recovery that brought markets back to new highs by 2013, this person's portfolio only reached maybe $800,000 because they had sold so many shares during the decline and those shares weren't around to participate in the recovery.

Compare this to someone who retired in 2009 at the market bottom with the same million dollars and the same $40,000 annual withdrawal. They started withdrawing just as markets began their recovery, experiencing strong returns in the first several years that grew their portfolio even while taking money out, and by 2013 they might have had $1,400,000 despite the same withdrawal amount and same average returns over the full period. The difference is entirely timing, with the 2007 retiree experiencing the worst sequence where losses came first and gains came later, while the 2009 retiree got the best sequence with gains first and any future losses coming after the portfolio had grown substantially.

The math works like this: Portfolio returns don't commute when we're making withdrawals, meaning 10% followed by negative 10% is not the same as negative 10% followed by 10% when we're pulling money out each year. Starting with $1 million, earning 10% gives us $1,100,000, withdrawing $40,000 leaves $1,060,000, then losing 10% brings us to $954,000. If we flip the order and lose 10% first to get $900,000, withdraw $40,000 to get $860,000, then earn 10% to reach $946,000, we end up $8,000 worse off from the same two returns in different order. This gap compounds over decades, turning small timing differences into six-figure variations in final outcomes.

The standard mitigation for sequence risk is holding several years of spending in cash or bonds so we don't have to sell stocks in a down market, usually three to five years of expenses in stable holdings that we can draw from while waiting for stocks to recover. Someone needing $40,000 per year might hold $200,000 in cash and short-term bonds covering five years of expenses, with the remaining $800,000 in stocks, and when markets decline they take withdrawals from the cash buffer rather than selling stocks at low prices. This preserves the stock holdings so they can participate in the eventual recovery, and as markets recover and stocks grow, we replenish the cash buffer by selling some gains at higher prices.

The cost of this insurance is the return drag from holding significant cash that earns nothing or minimal interest, and bonds that earn less than stocks over long periods. Someone holding $200,000 in cash and $800,000 in stocks misses out on stock gains on that $200,000, which over 30 years could be the difference between having $3 million and $2.4 million if stocks average 8% and cash averages 2%. The $600,000 difference might seem like an expensive insurance policy, but it must be weighed against the alternative of potentially running out of money if we retire into a severe bear market with no buffer.

A more dynamic approach adjusts withdrawals based on portfolio performance, spending less in down years and more in up years, which helps preserve capital during bad sequences but requires flexibility in spending that not everyone has. Someone who needs exactly $40,000 per year for fixed expenses including housing, healthcare, and basic living costs can't easily cut to $30,000 when the market drops, but someone with discretionary spending built into that $40,000 might skip the $10,000 vacation and reduce restaurant spending when the portfolio declines, eating into the cash buffer instead of selling stocks at a loss, then resuming higher spending once markets recover.

The guardrails method sets upper and lower bounds around the initial portfolio value adjusted for inflation, maybe 20% above and below, and adjusts spending only when we hit those guardrails rather than constantly tweaking based on small market movements. Starting with $1 million, the upper guardrail sits at $1,200,000 adjusted for inflation and the lower guardrail at $800,000 adjusted for inflation, and as long as the portfolio stays between these bounds we continue taking the same inflation-adjusted withdrawal. If the portfolio grows to exceed the upper guardrail, we increase spending by perhaps 10% to match the new wealth level. If it falls below the lower guardrail, we cut spending by 10% to preserve remaining capital.

This provides some inflation adjustment and upside participation while protecting against complete failure, and it prevents making constant small adjustments to spending every year based on market fluctuations that might reverse. The person whose portfolio grows from $1 million to $1,400,000 inflation-adjusted after five good years increases their withdrawal from the initial $40,000 to $44,000, enjoying some of the excess wealth. The person whose portfolio drops to $750,000 after a severe bear market cuts their withdrawal to $36,000, accepting reduced lifestyle to extend the portfolio's survival, then potentially increasing back to $40,000 or higher once markets recover and the portfolio crosses back above the lower guardrail.

Delaying Social Security to 70 provides additional sequence risk protection because the higher guaranteed benefit reduces the percentage of spending that comes from the portfolio, which means smaller withdrawals and less sensitivity to market timing. Someone with $1 million and a $2,480 per month Social Security benefit starting at 70 gets $29,760 annually from Social Security, and if they need $60,000 to live they only withdraw $30,240 from the portfolio, a 3% withdrawal rate that's quite safe. Someone who claimed Social Security at 62 and gets $1,400 per month receives only $16,800 annually, needing to withdraw $43,200 from the portfolio, a 4.3% withdrawal rate that's more vulnerable to sequence risk.

The higher withdrawal rate means selling more shares each year, which locks in larger losses during down markets and leaves fewer shares to participate in recoveries. In a scenario where the portfolio drops 40% in early retirement, the person withdrawing $30,240 annually can potentially avoid selling stocks by living on their cash buffer and Social Security, waiting for recovery without forcing sales at depressed prices. The person withdrawing $43,200 annually might exhaust their cash buffer more quickly and need to sell stocks while they're down, locking in losses that prevent full recovery even when markets eventually rebound.

Failure rate analysis at different portfolio sizes tells us something about feasibility and appropriate risk levels for our specific situation. With $500,000 saved and needing to withdraw $35,000 per year plus inflation, we're looking at a 7% initial withdrawal rate that produces failure rates around 40-50% over 30 years in historical simulations, meaning we're essentially gambling on whether we'll make it. The odds aren't quite as bad as a coin flip but they're close enough that this strategy should be rejected as too risky unless we have substantial other resources like a working spouse, guaranteed pension, or family wealth to fall back on.

At $800,000 needing the same $35,000 annually, we're at a 4.4% withdrawal rate that produces failure rates around 10-15% over 30 years depending on asset allocation and whether we adjust spending in down years. This level of risk might be acceptable for someone with good health, family support, and willingness to reduce spending if necessary, but it's too high for someone with no safety net or inflexible expenses. Increasing to $900,000 drops the withdrawal rate to 3.9% and cuts failure rates to maybe 5-8%, a meaningful improvement for relatively modest additional saving.

At $1,200,000 with the same $35,000 need, we're at 2.9% withdrawal rate and failure rates approach 1-2%, meaning we're highly likely to succeed and might even die with substantial wealth remaining. The question becomes whether the extra security is worth the additional years of work or reduced current spending needed to accumulate that $1,200,000 instead of retiring earlier with $800,000. Someone who works from 65 to 70 to build the portfolio from $800,000 to $1,200,000 trades five years of freedom for near-certainty of financial security throughout retirement, and the right answer depends on their health, job satisfaction, family situation, and tolerance for financial risk.

What failure actually means depends on the severity and timing, with complete portfolio depletion at different ages creating very different practical situations. Portfolio depletion at 90 after 30 years of retirement might feel acceptable if Social Security covers basic needs and we can downsize housing or move in with family, accepting reduced independence but maintaining basic security. We've had three decades of retirement and the depletion happens at an age where many people need assistance anyway, so the financial failure coincides with a natural transition point in life that might have happened regardless of money.

Depletion at 70 while still healthy and active creates a different kind of crisis, potentially forcing us back to work in our 70s when employment options are limited and health might not support full-time work, or into significant lifestyle reduction just when health problems start requiring more resources rather than less. Someone who depletes their portfolio at 70 faces potentially 15-20 more years living on Social Security alone, trying to cover increasing healthcare costs and basic living expenses with a fixed benefit that doesn't keep pace with medical inflation, and the gap between the retirement lifestyle they enjoyed from 60-70 and the restricted circumstances from 70 onward creates psychological and practical hardship.

The five-year period from 60 to 65 before Medicare eligibility is particularly dangerous for sequence risk because healthcare costs can spiral without the backstop of government insurance, and we're most vulnerable to portfolio depletion right when we need money to pay for individual health insurance. Someone who retires at 60 with $800,000 and experiences a 40% market decline in the first two years sees their portfolio drop to perhaps $500,000 after accounting for withdrawals, and they still need to pay $15,000-20,000 annually for health insurance until Medicare starts at 65. The combination of reduced portfolio and continuing high healthcare costs creates pressure to cut other spending or even return to work to get employer coverage, undermining the entire purpose of early retirement.

Success rates improve dramatically for people willing to work longer, both because the portfolio has more time to grow and because the retirement period shrinks, reducing the number of years the money must last. Someone retiring at 60 with $800,000 planning to live to 90 needs to fund 30 years, facing maybe 15% failure rate with a 4% withdrawal strategy. The same person retiring at 65 with $1,050,000 from five more years of contributions and growth needs to fund only 25 years, reducing failure rate to perhaps 5%. Retiring at 68 with $1,200,000 funding 22 years drops failure rate below 2%, transforming a risky strategy into a quite safe one through three years of additional work.

The marginal benefit of each additional year of work increases as we approach safe withdrawal territory, because we're simultaneously increasing the numerator through contributions and growth while decreasing the denominator through fewer years of required funding. Working from 67 to 68 might add $80,000 to the portfolio and reduce retirement length by one year, having larger impact than working from 62 to 63 because we're closer to the safe zone and each improvement matters more. This argues for working at least until the point where failure rates drop below our personal tolerance level, even if that means working longer than we originally hoped.

Flexibility in retirement spending creates options that fixed spending doesn't allow, because we can respond to portfolio performance rather than blindly following a predetermined withdrawal schedule into potential depletion. Someone who spent $50,000 in year one when the portfolio was at $1 million might choose to spend only $45,000 in year five if the portfolio has dropped to $850,000, cutting discretionary expenses to preserve capital during a downturn, then resuming $50,000 or higher spending once the portfolio recovers above $1 million. This responsiveness to market conditions reduces failure rates substantially compared to rigid spending that continues regardless of portfolio performance.

The challenge of flexible spending is distinguishing between temporary market volatility that will reverse and permanent portfolio decline that signals we're on track to fail, because cutting spending every time the market drops 10% creates unnecessary lifestyle disruption while waiting too long to cut spending when we're genuinely on a path to depletion can make the eventual cuts more severe. Someone whose portfolio drops from $1 million to $900,000 in a single year might reasonably wait to see if it recovers before adjusting spending, but someone whose portfolio declines from $1 million to $900,000 to $800,000 to $750,000 over four years needs to recognize this isn't temporary volatility but a structural problem requiring spending reductions.

The spending flexibility also depends on what portion of our budget is truly discretionary versus fixed. Someone spending $60,000 annually with $45,000 in fixed costs for housing, healthcare, utilities, food, and insurance can only cut the remaining $15,000 discretionary spending, limiting downward adjustment to 25% of total spending. Someone spending $60,000 with $35,000 in fixed costs has $25,000 in discretionary room, allowing cuts of up to 40% if necessary. The person with higher fixed costs has less ability to respond to portfolio stress and needs higher success rates from the start, because their flexibility to cut spending is constrained by structural obligations.

Part-time work in early retirement provides both supplemental income and sequence risk protection by reducing portfolio withdrawals during the vulnerable first decade. Someone who works 20 hours per week earning $20,000 annually can reduce portfolio withdrawals by that amount, turning a $40,000 withdrawal into a $20,000 withdrawal and dropping the withdrawal rate from 4% to 2% while they're working. This part-time income continues until they decide to stop or until health makes it impossible, providing several years of much lower portfolio stress during the period when sequence risk is highest, then they transition to full portfolio funding once the dangerous early years have passed.

The combination of part-time work, flexible spending, Social Security delay, and appropriate asset allocation creates a layered defense against failure that's more robust than any single strategy alone. Someone who works part-time from 60-67 earning $20,000 annually, adjusts spending based on portfolio performance, delays Social Security to 70, and maintains a bond buffer for down markets has protected themselves against most failure scenarios short of complete market collapse or catastrophic health costs. Each layer addresses different risks and provides redundancy so that if one protection fails another can compensate.

Monte Carlo simulation results should inform our planning but not dictate it mechanically, because the simulations make assumptions about return distributions, inflation patterns, and our behavior that might not match reality. Historical returns might not predict future returns if we're entering a period of lower growth or higher inflation than the past century, and our actual behavior under stress might differ from the planned behavior we input into the model. Someone who plans to cut spending by 20% in down markets might find they can't actually do this when faced with the reality of reduced lifestyle, or they might discover they can cut more than they thought by making changes they didn't anticipate.

We can use simulation results to identify which variables matter most for our specific situation, revealing whether our success rate is most sensitive to withdrawal rate, asset allocation, retirement length, or spending flexibility. Someone whose success rate jumps from 75% to 95% by reducing withdrawal rate from 4.5% to 4% should probably reduce withdrawal rate, while someone whose success rate only improves from 90% to 92% with the same change might reasonably keep the higher withdrawal rate and enjoy the extra spending. The sensitivity analysis tells us where to focus our adjustments for maximum impact on success probability.

The honest assessment of failure risk requires combining the quantitative analysis from simulations with qualitative judgment about our circumstances, resources, and adaptability. A 10% failure rate might be acceptable for someone with substantial home equity they could tap in emergency, adult children who are financially stable and could provide support, and willingness to move to a cheaper location if needed. The same 10% failure rate is unacceptable for someone with no backup resources, no family support, inflexible location due to health needs, and unwillingness or inability to reduce spending significantly.

We should also consider the asymmetry of outcomes where the cost of being too conservative is dying with money we could have enjoyed, while the cost of being too aggressive is poverty in old age when we're least able to work or recover. These costs aren't equal, and most people should prefer erring on the side of too much saving and too much caution rather than too little, because the downside of excessive conservatism is having money to leave to heirs or donate while the downside of excessive risk is destitution. Someone who saved $1.2 million instead of $900,000 and dies with $400,000 remaining has paid an opportunity cost in reduced current consumption, but someone who saved $900,000 instead of $1.2 million and runs out of money at 82 faces genuine hardship with no good options.

The failure rate we can accept depends ultimately on our tolerance for uncertainty, our backup options if things go wrong, and our ability to adjust spending and lifestyle in response to portfolio stress. There's no universally correct answer, but there are situations where the numbers clearly indicate we're taking too much risk or being unnecessarily conservative, and we should pay attention to these signals rather than proceeding blindly with a plan that the analysis shows is likely to fail or that requires far more saving than necessary for our goals.

Monte Carlo analysis tells us the probability of success across thousands of simulated futures. But the average of those outcomes doesn't matter as much as what we'd do if we landed in one of the bad ones. Understanding failure modes in the abstract is useful. Knowing whether our own specific situation is on solid ground, marginal ground, or borrowed time is something else entirely.

What the Math Says

Some of us are not going to be able to retire in the traditional sense of stopping work completely at 65 or even 70, and facing that reality clearly beats pretending otherwise until we're 68 with $200,000 saved and no idea what to do next. The honest assessment starts with current age, current savings, realistic saving rate going forward, expected Social Security benefit, and desired retirement age, then works through the math without wishful thinking about investment returns or sudden windfalls that probably aren't coming. We need to see whether the trajectory we're on leads to successful retirement or whether it leads to working until we physically can't anymore and then scraping by on Social Security alone.

Someone who is 45 years old with $50,000 saved, earning $60,000 per year, and able to save 15% annually faces specific mathematical constraints that determine what's possible. Fifteen percent of $60,000 is $9,000 per year, and saving this amount from 45 to 67 while the existing $50,000 grows at 7% annually produces a portfolio of about $440,000 by traditional retirement age. Social Security benefit will be reduced because of the late career start and lower lifetime earnings compared to someone who worked continuously from their 20s, probably landing around $1,800 per month or $21,600 per year. The portfolio generates $17,600 at 4% withdrawal rate, for total retirement income of $39,200 per year.

This person cannot maintain a $60,000 per year lifestyle in retirement, full stop, and the question becomes what combination of adjustments makes the math work. They're currently living on roughly $51,000 after the $9,000 in retirement savings, though taxes reduce this further to maybe $43,000-45,000 in actual take-home pay, so their current lifestyle is already well below what they'll need to maintain in retirement if they continue at the $39,200 income level. The gap between current working lifestyle and retirement income is smaller than it first appears, but it's still a gap, and they need to decide whether to work longer, save more, accept lower retirement spending, plan part-time work in retirement, or move to a cheaper location.

Working longer is the most obvious lever though not always the most available one since layoffs and health problems force early retirement more often than we'd like to admit. Each additional year of work accomplishes three things simultaneously: one more year of contributions adding to the portfolio, one more year of investment growth on the existing balance, and one fewer year the portfolio needs to fund. Working from 67 to 72 instead of retiring at 67 might increase the portfolio from $440,000 to $620,000 through the combination of five more years of $9,000 contributions growing at 7% and five more years of growth on the existing balance.

Social Security at 72 isn't an option because benefits max out at age 70 regardless of when we claim, but working until 72 and claiming at 70 gets us to the maximum benefit while providing two more years of income and portfolio growth after benefits start. The delayed benefit might increase from $1,800 per month at 67 to $2,250 per month at 70, an extra $450 monthly or $5,400 annually, and this increase lasts for life, providing larger income in our 80s and 90s when other resources might be depleted. Combined with the larger portfolio of $620,000 generating $24,800 at 4% withdrawal, total retirement income reaches $51,000 annually, much closer to sustainable than the $39,200 we were looking at with retirement at 67.

The five extra years of work from 67 to 72 transformed an inadequate retirement into a workable one, but those five years represent a significant portion of remaining healthy life, and someone in poor health or with a physically demanding job might not be able to work that long. The trade is real: five years of working versus 15-20 years of financial security in retirement, and the right choice depends on health, job satisfaction, family circumstances, and whether we can tolerate the work for those additional years without breaking down physically or mentally.

Increasing the saving rate provides another path to adequacy, though it requires reducing current lifestyle to fund higher retirement contributions. Someone currently saving 15% of $60,000 might increase to 25%, saving $15,000 annually instead of $9,000, which means living on $6,000 less each year while working but accumulating significantly more by retirement age. The $15,000 annual contributions from 45 to 67 grow the portfolio from the projected $440,000 to about $690,000, and combined with the same $21,600 Social Security provides total retirement income of $49,200, much better than the original $39,200 though still below current pre-retirement spending.

The challenge of increasing saving rate is that it reduces current standard of living during working years when we might have children at home, aging parents needing help, or other expenses that feel non-negotiable, and saving an extra $6,000 per year means cutting $500 per month from current spending, which might come from eating out less, taking cheaper vacations, driving an older car, or living in a smaller house. These cuts are real and affect quality of life now in exchange for better outcomes later, and each person must decide whether the trade makes sense given their circumstances and values.

The combination of working longer and saving more creates even larger improvements through the compounding effects of more contributions over more years with fewer years to fund. Working until 70 instead of 67 while saving $15,000 instead of $9,000 grows the portfolio to about $830,000, generating $33,200 annually at 4% withdrawal plus $24,800 from Social Security delayed to 70, for total retirement income of $58,000. This approaches current pre-retirement spending levels and represents a retirement that's financially sustainable even if not luxurious, achieved through three extra years of work and living on $6,000 less annually while working.

Reducing retirement spending expectations offers a third adjustment that doesn't require working longer or saving more but does require accepting a different lifestyle in retirement than we might have imagined. Someone planning to spend $50,000 per year who realizes they can only generate $39,200 needs to find $10,800 in annual spending cuts, which might come from downsizing housing from a $1,800 monthly payment to $1,000, reducing from $400 to $200 monthly for entertainment and dining out, eliminating a $5,000 annual vacation budget, and cutting miscellaneous discretionary spending that adds up to several thousand per year.

The difficulty of spending cuts depends on what portion of current spending is truly discretionary versus fixed by circumstances. Someone spending $60,000 annually might have $40,000 in relatively fixed costs for housing, healthcare, food, utilities, insurance, and basic transportation, with only $20,000 in discretionary spending that could be cut. Reducing total spending from $50,000 to $39,200 requires cutting $10,800, and if discretionary spending is only $20,000, this represents cutting more than half of all discretionary expenses, which might mean no vacations, minimal entertainment, rare restaurant meals, and a generally restricted lifestyle that feels like deprivation rather than retirement.

Geographic arbitrage means moving to where money goes further, whether that's from expensive coastal cities to cheaper inland areas, from high-tax states to no-tax states, or from the United States to lower-cost countries abroad. The math can be compelling when housing costs drop from $2,500 per month to $1,200, or when moving from California to Florida eliminates $3,000-4,000 in state income tax annually, or when property taxes fall from $8,000 to $2,000 per year. Someone who needs $50,000 to live in Boston might need only $35,000 in Pensacola for the same quality of life, and at 4% withdrawal rate this means $1,250,000 required savings versus $875,000, a difference of $375,000 that might represent the difference between retirement being feasible and impossible.

The hidden costs of moving include the actual expense of relocating which might run $10,000-20,000 for a cross-country move with household goods, the emotional cost of leaving friends and community built over decades, the potential isolation and loneliness in a new location where we have no connections, the reduced access to specialized healthcare and cultural amenities that larger cities provide, and the risk that we'll need to move back after several years if health declines and we need family support, paying moving costs twice and losing the benefit of the initial move. These costs are hard to quantify but very real, and someone moving from San Francisco to Pensacola at 62 might find themselves moving back to San Francisco at 75 when they need to be near children, having spent 13 years in Florida but ending up back in the expensive location anyway.

The assessment of whether geographic moves make sense depends on strength of current community ties, proximity to family, health status and likelihood of needing family help, willingness to build new social connections in our 60s or 70s, and tolerance for different cultural environments and climates. Someone with weak ties to their current expensive location, adult children scattered across the country, good health, and adventurous personality might thrive in a new cheaper location, while someone with deep community roots, children and grandchildren nearby, health concerns requiring specialist care, and preference for familiar surroundings might be miserable anywhere else regardless of the cost savings.

Part-time work in retirement changes both the math and the psychology of sustainability by reducing portfolio withdrawals and providing structure and purpose that pure leisure retirement sometimes lacks. Twenty hours per week at $20 per hour generates $20,000 per year pre-tax, maybe $16,000 after taxes, and this income can either supplement Social Security to reduce portfolio withdrawals or can cover all discretionary spending while Social Security and portfolio withdrawals handle fixed costs. Someone with $440,000 saved and $21,600 Social Security who works part-time earning $16,000 can live on $37,600 without touching the portfolio at all, letting it continue growing through their 60s and early 70s until they can't or don't want to work anymore.

The viability of part-time work depends on whether we can find employment at 65-75 that pays reasonably and doesn't destroy our bodies or mental health, which varies enormously by profession, location, and individual circumstances. Someone with marketable skills in consulting, accounting, writing, or other knowledge work might easily find part-time arrangements that pay well and offer flexibility, while someone whose career was in manufacturing, retail, or physically demanding service work might struggle to find part-time options that are both available and tolerable. We also need to be realistic about whether we'll want to work in our 70s even if we can, because the job that seems fine at 67 might feel intolerable at 74 when health declines and energy wanes.

The combination approach uses all available levers rather than relying on just one adjustment to close the gap between what we have and what we need. Work until 69 instead of 65 for four extra years of contributions and growth, move to a state with lower cost of living and no income tax, plan on part-time work earning $15,000 annually until 75, and reduce discretionary spending by $5,000 per year, and suddenly the impossible math becomes workable. Someone who couldn't retire at 65 with $500,000 saved and $50,000 spending needs can retire at 69 with $700,000 saved, $40,000 spending needs due to the move, $15,000 part-time income until 75, and Social Security of $2,100 per month at 69.

The combined strategy means working four more years, accepting a different location than we might prefer, continuing to work part-time for six years after retirement from the primary career, and living more frugally than we hoped, but it's a retirement that's actually sustainable rather than a fantasy that leads to depletion at 78. This isn't the retirement we imagined when we were 30, but it beats working full-time until we physically can't anymore or running out of money while we're still alive and facing the choice between homelessness and complete dependence on children who might not be able to help.

Late starters who reach 45 or 50 with minimal retirement savings face particularly brutal math that requires either dramatic lifestyle changes or acceptance that traditional retirement won't happen. Someone who is 50 with $30,000 saved and earning $70,000 annually can contribute the maximum $30,500 per year including catch-up contributions from age 50 onward, and doing this for 17 years until 67 produces a portfolio of about $870,000, which generates $34,800 at 4% withdrawal plus Social Security of maybe $2,100 per month or $25,200 annually for total income of $60,000 in retirement.

This scenario requires saving $30,500 per year on $70,000 earnings, which is 44% of gross income and probably 55-60% of after-tax income, leaving roughly $30,000-35,000 to live on while working. Most people cannot maintain this saving rate for 17 consecutive years, especially if they have children, aging parents, or other obligations that require money. The more realistic scenario is saving 20-25% of gross income, maybe $14,000-17,500 per year, which produces a portfolio of $510,000-630,000 by 67, generating $20,400-25,200 annually plus the same $25,200 Social Security for total retirement income of $45,600-50,400.

This late starter earning $70,000 and living on perhaps $55,000 after retirement savings and taxes cannot maintain that lifestyle in retirement on $45,600-50,400, and they face the choice of working until 72-75 to accumulate more, drastically reducing retirement spending through geographic moves and lifestyle cuts, planning to work part-time throughout retirement, or accepting that they'll never fully retire and will need to work at least part-time until health makes it impossible. These are hard choices with no good options, and they result from either starting retirement saving too late, saving too little during working years, or experiencing setbacks like job loss, divorce, or medical expenses that depleted savings.

The assessment for late starters must be particularly realistic because they have less time for optimistic assumptions to play out and less room to recover from mistakes. Someone who is 50 with minimal savings and saves aggressively for five years then stops can't make up the lost ground, while someone who is 30 with minimal savings has 35 years for compound growth to work. The 50-year-old needs to save more per year, work longer before retirement, and probably accept lower retirement income than someone who started earlier, and wishful thinking about market returns solving the problem or inheritance appearing creates dangerous false hope that leads to worse outcomes.

People who won't be able to retire traditionally need alternative plans that acknowledge the reality rather than ignoring it until the money runs out. This might mean planning to work part-time indefinitely, accepting that retirement means reduced hours rather than no hours, or it might mean positioning ourselves for work we can do in our 70s like consulting in our field, teaching, or service work that's not physically demanding. It might mean moving to a much cheaper location where part-time work plus Social Security plus a small portfolio can sustain us, or moving in with adult children if they're willing and able to help, or building a living situation with friends where we can share housing costs and support each other.

The honest assessment requires looking at real numbers rather than hopes, running the actual calculations with our specific savings, age, and income rather than using generic rules that might not apply, and accepting the results even when they're disappointing. Someone who is 55 with $150,000 saved and earning $50,000 annually needs to know that retiring at 65 with $450,000 and Social Security of $1,700 per month means total retirement income around $38,000, and they cannot live on this if they currently need $45,000 to cover expenses. Ignoring this gap and retiring anyway leads to running out of money at 75 or 80, while acknowledging it now allows for planning around working longer, saving more, or reducing retirement spending expectations.

We should also be honest about the risks and uncertainties that could derail even solid plans, including forced early retirement through layoffs or health problems, lower investment returns than historical averages if we're entering a period of below-average growth, higher inflation than projected if we experience sustained price increases, unexpected health costs that drain savings before retirement, or Social Security benefit cuts if Congress doesn't fix the system's funding gap. Someone retiring right at the edge of feasibility with no margin for error is vulnerable to any of these risks derailing their retirement, while someone with significant cushion can absorb most normal setbacks without destroying their plan.

The margin of safety we need depends on our backup options and adaptability to changing circumstances. Someone with home equity they could tap through a reverse mortgage, adult children who are financially stable and could help, or willingness to move to a much cheaper location if needed can accept smaller cushions than someone with no backup resources, children who can't help, and inflexible location requirements due to health needs. The difference isn't about being conservative versus aggressive with planning but about having realistic fallback positions versus having no options if the primary plan fails.

Building flexibility into retirement plans acknowledges that we can't predict the future perfectly and that adjustments will probably be necessary regardless of how well we plan. Someone who retires with a plan to spend $45,000 annually but stays alert to portfolio performance and willing to cut spending if needed can respond to problems before they become catastrophic, reducing to $40,000 or $38,000 if markets perform poorly or healthcare costs exceed projections. Someone who retires with a fixed spending plan and refuses to adjust regardless of circumstances is setting themselves up for eventual forced cuts that are more severe and come at worse times than voluntary early cuts would have been.

The psychological challenge of honest assessment is that it might reveal we're further behind than we wanted to believe or that retirement isn't possible in the form we imagined, and confronting this reality requires accepting disappointment and adjusting expectations rather than clinging to pleasant fiction. Someone who hoped to retire at 60 and travel extensively might learn they need to work until 68 and live modestly, and the gap between the hoped-for retirement and the realistic one creates grief that must be processed. Avoiding the assessment and maintaining unrealistic hopes feels better in the short term but leads to worse outcomes when reality eventually forces confrontation at age 67 with insufficient savings.

We can choose to do the assessment at 45 or 50 when there's still time to make major adjustments, or we can avoid it and discover the problem at 65 when options are limited to working longer or accepting poverty. The earlier assessment is uncomfortable but useful because it shows us what adjustments are needed while we have time to implement them, whether that's increasing saving rate, planning to work longer, preparing for geographic moves, developing part-time work options, or some combination. The later assessment is devastating because it reveals problems when we can't solve them adequately, leaving us to choose among bad options with no good path forward.

The question we must answer is whether we're on track for the retirement we want, and if not, what specific changes we need to make to get on track, and whether we're willing to make those changes. Someone earning $80,000 with $300,000 saved at age 52 who wants to retire at 65 with $55,000 annual spending needs to accumulate about $1,100,000 by 65 after accounting for Social Security of $2,300 per month or $27,600 annually. They can probably get there by maximizing contributions at $30,500 per year for 13 years, but this requires living on $49,500 before taxes or about $38,000 after taxes, which might mean significant lifestyle cuts now to fund adequate retirement later.

If they're unwilling or unable to make those cuts, they need to adjust either retirement age or retirement spending expectations, retiring at 68 instead of 65 to accumulate more and reduce years of funding needed, or accepting $48,000 in retirement spending instead of $55,000 through downsizing housing and cutting discretionary expenses. The assessment reveals these trade-offs clearly so we can make informed choices rather than drifting toward retirement with vague hopes that somehow it will work out.

The final piece of honest assessment is asking what happens if we're wrong about key assumptions like market returns, inflation, longevity, or health costs, and whether our plan survives moderate deviations from expectations. Someone retiring with exactly enough money assuming 7% returns and 3% inflation who encounters 5% returns and 4% inflation will fail, while someone retiring with 20% more than the minimum required can probably weather these variations. The question is whether we're building plans that work only under favorable assumptions or plans that survive normal bad luck and moderate estimation errors.

The retirement we can actually have might be less impressive than the retirement we wish we could have, and the honest assessment forces us to acknowledge this gap and decide how to respond. We can work longer to close the gap through more saving and fewer years of funding needed, we can reduce retirement spending expectations to match what we can actually afford, we can plan ongoing part-time work to supplement savings and Social Security, we can move to cheaper locations to stretch our money further, or we can accept that we're going to run short in our 80s and plan for what that means practically. What we can't do successfully is ignore the gap and hope it resolves itself, because it won't, and the later we confront it the worse our options become.

The honest assessment identifies the gap. The question is how to close it — through more contributions, more years of work, lower spending, or some combination. Most of that closing happens inside specific accounts that the tax code has built for exactly this purpose. The first and most powerful of those accounts is the one most people have access to but rarely optimize.

The Accounts at Work

A 401k is an employer-sponsored retirement account named after section 401(k) of the Internal Revenue Code that created it in 1978, and it works by letting us contribute money directly from our paycheck before income taxes get calculated, reducing our taxable income in the year we contribute while the money grows without being taxed on dividends or capital gains until we eventually withdraw it in retirement. The employer sets up the plan with a financial institution like Fidelity or Vanguard, chooses which investment options to offer from that institution's menu, and handles the payroll deduction that moves money from our gross pay into the retirement account before calculating how much we owe in federal and state income taxes.

For someone earning $60,000 who contributes $10,000 to their 401k, their taxable income drops to $50,000, saving them roughly $2,400 in federal taxes if they're in the 24% bracket plus whatever state taxes apply, and that $10,000 plus the tax savings goes into the account to grow through stock and bond investments we choose from the plan's options. The trade is simple: we get tax savings now and tax-deferred growth for decades, but when we withdraw the money in retirement, every dollar comes out as ordinary income taxed at whatever our rate is then, including both our original contributions and all the growth.

The 403b works functionally identically to the 401k but exists for employees of tax-exempt organizations under section 403(b) of the tax code, meaning teachers, hospital workers, employees of charities and religious organizations, and people working for universities get 403b plans instead of 401k plans. The contribution limits are the same, the tax treatment is the same, and the basic strategy is the same, though historically 403b plans offered annuity contracts as investment options rather than mutual funds, and some plans still carry those legacy annuity options with high fees that we should avoid in favor of low-cost index funds when available.

The 457 plan serves government employees and some nonprofit workers under section 457 of the tax code, and while it looks similar to 401k and 403b with the same contribution limits and tax-deferred growth, it has one major difference that matters for early retirement: withdrawals from a 457 can happen penalty-free as soon as we leave the job, regardless of our age. Someone who leaves government employment at 52 can access their 457 money immediately without the 10% early withdrawal penalty that would apply to 401k or 403b money, though they still pay ordinary income tax on the withdrawals. This makes 457 plans particularly valuable for people planning early retirement, since the money becomes available whenever we stop working rather than being locked up until 59.5.

The 401k contribution limit in 2024 sits at $23,000 for people under 50, and an additional $7,500 catch-up contribution becomes available at age 50, bringing the total to $30,500. These numbers increase occasionally with inflation adjustments, and they represent the maximum we can put in regardless of salary, though obviously someone making $40,000 can't save $23,000 without living on $17,000 before taxes, which isn't possible once we account for income taxes, payroll taxes, housing, food, and basic living expenses that don't disappear just because we're trying to save aggressively.

The practical limit on contributions is what we can actually live without, which for most people is somewhere between 10% and 20% of gross income, meaning someone earning $80,000 might realistically contribute $8,000 to $16,000 annually even though the legal limit is $23,000. Someone earning $150,000 has more room to hit the maximum contribution while still having enough left over to live on, and this creates one of many ways that higher earners have easier paths to retirement than people earning moderate incomes who must choose between adequate saving and adequate current lifestyle.

Employer match is free money with an immediate 100% return, assuming we stay employed long enough to vest, which typically takes three to five years depending on the company's vesting schedule. Someone earning $60,000 with a 50% match on the first 6% of contributions gets $1,800 per year in employer contributions by contributing $3,600 themselves, and failing to contribute at least enough to get the full match is leaving that money on the table. The match doesn't count against our personal contribution limit, so we can still put in the full $23,000 on top of whatever the employer contributes, and someone fortunate enough to work for a company with generous matching might get $10,000 or more in employer contributions annually if they maximize their own contributions.

Vesting schedules determine when employer contributions actually belong to us rather than being subject to forfeiture if we leave the job, and these schedules vary from immediate vesting where we own the match right away to graded vesting over three to six years where we own increasing percentages each year to cliff vesting where we own nothing until hitting a specific number of years and then own everything. Someone with a four-year cliff vesting schedule who leaves after three years loses all employer contributions made during those three years, potentially giving up $15,000 or more in forfeited match, while someone who stays until year four gets to keep everything including all the growth on those contributions.

The vesting cliff creates golden handcuffs that keep people in jobs longer than they might otherwise stay, and someone who is unhappy at work but six months away from a vesting cliff faces the difficult choice of leaving immediately and forfeiting maybe $20,000 in unvested match or staying six more months in a situation that's making them miserable to capture that money. The right answer depends on how bad the job situation is, how much money is at stake, and what alternative opportunities exist, but it's worth knowing the vesting schedule before making job change decisions that could forfeit significant accumulated match.

Our own contributions vest immediately because it's our money that we put in, and we can always take those contributions and their growth when we leave a job, but employer match follows the vesting schedule and might be partially or completely forfeited depending on tenure. The actual mechanics of what happens to unvested money varies by plan, with some returning it to the employer to reduce their future matching costs and others reallocating it among remaining participants, but either way we don't get to keep it if we leave before vesting.

Roth versus Traditional refers to when we pay taxes on the money: Traditional means we get a tax deduction now when we contribute but pay taxes later when we withdraw, while Roth means we pay taxes now on the money before contributing but then never pay taxes again on either the contributions or the growth when we withdraw in retirement. Most 401k plans now offer both options, letting us choose for each contribution whether to put it in the Traditional side or the Roth side, and the choice comes down to whether we think our tax rate in retirement will be higher or lower than our current rate, though the real answer involves more complexity than that simple framing suggests.

Traditional 401k contributions come out of our paycheck before taxes get calculated, reducing our taxable income this year, so someone earning $80,000 who contributes $20,000 to Traditional 401k only pays income tax on $60,000, and that $20,000 grows tax-deferred until we withdraw it in retirement when it gets taxed as ordinary income. Roth 401k contributions happen after taxes, so we pay tax on the full $80,000 now, but the $20,000 contribution and all its growth come out tax-free in retirement, and we never pay taxes on any of it again. Traditional contributions reduce our taxable income now, so someone in the 24% bracket saves $5,520 in current-year taxes on a $23,000 contribution, but they'll pay ordinary income tax on all withdrawals in retirement. Roth contributions get taxed now but grow and withdraw tax-free forever, and the tax-free nature in retirement provides flexibility for managing taxable income to optimize ACA subsidies, avoid Medicare IRMAA surcharges, and minimize Social Security benefit taxation.

The conventional wisdom says use Traditional when young and earning less, switch to Roth as income rises, but this ignores the reality that many people's income peaks in their 40s and 50s when they're in their highest tax brackets, and retirement income might be lower but it's not zero. Someone retiring with $1.5 million in Traditional 401k faces required minimum distributions starting at 73 that could push them into higher brackets than they expected, while having some money in Roth provides options for managing that tax burden. A mix of Traditional and Roth gives flexibility that pure Traditional or pure Roth doesn't provide, because we can choose which account to withdraw from in any given year based on our tax situation, taking Traditional money in low-income years to fill up lower brackets and Roth money in high-income years to avoid bracket creep.

Someone in the 12% bracket now who expects to be in the 12% or 22% bracket in retirement should probably use Traditional contributions to get the deduction now, gambling that they won't end up in a much higher bracket later. Someone in the 32% or 35% bracket now who expects to be in the 22% or 24% bracket in retirement should definitely use Traditional to get the larger deduction at high rates and pay tax later at lower rates. Someone in the 24% bracket now who's uncertain about future tax rates might split contributions between Traditional and Roth, getting some deduction now while also building tax-free Roth money for flexibility later.

The wild card is future tax rates set by Congress, which could increase across the board if the federal government needs more revenue, potentially making today's 24% bracket become tomorrow's 30% bracket and turning the Traditional contribution strategy into a mistake. We can't predict future tax policy with certainty, which argues for having money in both Traditional and Roth accounts to hedge against different scenarios, and the diversification of tax treatment provides optionality in retirement that pure Traditional savers don't have.

In-service withdrawals and rollovers depend on specific plan rules, and many plans allow rollovers to IRA while still employed, though some require waiting until age 59.5 or later. This matters for people doing backdoor Roth conversions who need to get pre-tax IRA money back into their 401k to avoid the pro-rata rule, and it matters for people who want more investment options than their 401k provides and can get lower fees through IRA index funds. Someone whose 401k charges 1% expense ratios on actively managed funds when they could get 0.05% index funds in an IRA has strong incentive to roll money out if the plan allows, potentially saving thousands per year in fees that compound over decades into six-figure differences in final portfolio value.

The ability to roll money from IRA back into 401k while employed solves the backdoor Roth problem for high earners who have accumulated pre-tax IRA money and want to start doing annual backdoor Roth contributions. Without the ability to move pre-tax IRA money somewhere else, the pro-rata rule makes backdoor Roth contributions partially taxable and defeats the purpose, but rolling that pre-tax money into the current 401k clears out the IRA so the backdoor Roth conversion can happen without triggering pro-rata taxation. Not all plans accept incoming rollovers, so we need to check plan documents or ask HR whether this option exists.

Leaving a job creates a rollover decision that's mostly straightforward but has some nuances worth considering. Rolling the old 401k to an IRA gives complete control over investments and fees, and it consolidates accounts into fewer statements and fewer passwords to remember, which matters more as we accumulate accounts from multiple employers over a 30-40 year career. Someone who has worked for five different companies might have five old 401k accounts scattered across different providers, and rolling them all into a single IRA at Vanguard or Fidelity simplifies management and makes it easier to implement a coherent investment strategy across the entire portfolio.

Keeping money in the old 401k makes sense if the plan has excellent low-cost options we can't access elsewhere, like institutional index funds with expense ratios below 0.02% that aren't available to retail IRA investors, or if we left the job at 55 or later and might need penalty-free access before 59.5 under the Rule of 55. Someone who retires at 57 and rolls their 401k to IRA loses the ability to access that money penalty-free until 59.5, but keeping it in the 401k preserves the Rule of 55 access for those two years, and this might be worth the inconvenience of maintaining the old account.

Rolling to a new employer's 401k works when the new plan is good and we want everything in one place, but it's usually the least common choice because IRAs offer more flexibility for most people. The new plan might have limited investment options or high fees, and consolidating into that environment rather than a self-directed IRA gives up control we might want later. The exception is someone doing backdoor Roth conversions who needs to keep their IRA accounts clear of pre-tax money, in which case rolling everything into the 401k and keeping all retirement money in employer plans makes the backdoor Roth strategy work cleanly.

The rollover itself requires paperwork from both the old 401k provider and the receiving IRA custodian or new 401k, and we want to do a direct rollover where the money moves from one institution to the other without passing through our hands. The indirect rollover where the old 401k sends us a check and we have 60 days to deposit it into the new account creates withholding complications and the risk that we'll miss the deadline and turn the distribution into a taxable event, and there's no benefit to indirect rollover that justifies these risks when direct rollover is available.

Investment choices within a 401k are limited to whatever menu the employer and plan provider have selected, and this ranges from excellent plans with dozens of low-cost index funds covering every asset class to terrible plans with only high-fee actively managed funds and company stock. Someone whose plan offers total market index funds, international index funds, and bond index funds all with expense ratios under 0.1% has everything they need to build a complete portfolio, while someone whose plan offers only actively managed funds with 1% expense ratios and limited category coverage should contribute enough to get employer match but probably shouldn't contribute beyond that if they have access to IRA or other lower-cost options.

The three-fund portfolio approach works well in most 401k accounts and involves holding a U.S. total stock market fund, an international total stock market fund, and a total bond market fund in proportions that match our age and risk tolerance. Someone who is 40 might hold 60% U.S. stocks, 20% international stocks, and 20% bonds, rebalancing annually to maintain these ratios as market movements push the allocation off target. This simple approach captures most of the available diversification benefit without requiring exotic investments or constant trading, and it works fine for accumulation even though we might want more sophistication in retirement when tax-efficient withdrawal strategies matter more.

Company stock in a 401k is generally a bad idea because it concentrates risk in a single company that also happens to be our employer, meaning both our income and our retirement savings depend on the same company's success. Someone who works for a company that fails loses their job and watches their 401k balance evaporate simultaneously, creating devastating outcomes that diversified portfolios avoid, and even if the company doesn't fail, holding large amounts of its stock creates volatility and company-specific risk that doesn't get compensated with higher expected returns. The Enron employees who had their 401k accounts heavily weighted toward Enron stock learned this lesson catastrophically when the company collapsed and their retirement savings disappeared along with their jobs.

Some employers strongly encourage or even require company stock holdings in their 401k match, contributing the match in company shares rather than cash, and while we can often sell these shares immediately and reinvest in diversified funds, some plans impose holding periods that force us to keep the company stock for months or years. This is a form of forced concentration that benefits the company by stabilizing the share price and creating employee loyalty but harms employees by exposing them to company-specific risk they shouldn't be taking with retirement money.

The loan feature that many 401k plans offer lets us borrow from our own account and pay ourselves back with interest, and while this sounds appealing during emergencies, it creates problems if we leave the job before repaying because the outstanding balance becomes a taxable distribution subject to taxes and potentially the 10% early withdrawal penalty. Someone who borrows $20,000 from their 401k and then gets laid off six months later faces immediate tax on that $20,000 plus $2,000 penalty if they're under 59.5, turning what seemed like a convenient loan into an expensive forced distribution. The repayment requirement also means we're paying ourselves back with after-tax money that will be taxed again when withdrawn in retirement, creating double taxation on the loan amount.

Hardship withdrawals provide access to 401k money before 59.5 without the loan requirement, but they trigger taxes and the 10% penalty, and they're only available for specific qualifying events like preventing foreclosure, paying medical expenses, or covering funeral costs. Someone facing financial emergency might have no choice but to take a hardship withdrawal, but it should be the last resort after exhausting other options like personal loans, home equity lines, or reducing expenses, because the taxes and penalty consume 30-40% of the withdrawal and the money comes out of retirement savings permanently, reducing future security for current crisis management.

The automatic enrollment features that many employers have implemented help people who would otherwise never sign up for the 401k, but the default contribution rates are often too low, like 3% of salary, and the default investments are often target-date funds that might be fine or might have high fees depending on the plan. Someone who gets automatically enrolled at 3% contributions when they could afford 10% misses out on years of higher contributions that compound into significant differences in final portfolio value, and the automatic annual increases that some plans implement typically max out at 6-10% rather than pushing people toward the contribution limits.

We need to actively manage our 401k rather than just accepting defaults, increasing contribution rates to whatever level we can sustain, checking expense ratios on available investment options and choosing the lowest-cost funds that provide needed diversification, and rebalancing at least annually to maintain our target allocation rather than letting successful investments take over the portfolio. Someone who set their 401k allocation to 60% stocks and 40% bonds in 2009 and never rebalanced probably has 80% or more in stocks now after a decade-plus of strong equity returns, creating more risk than they intended and exposing them to larger losses in the next bear market.

The administrative details of 401k plans include beneficiary designations that determine who gets the money when we die, and we need to keep these updated after major life events like marriage, divorce, or births. The beneficiary designation overrides our will, so someone who divorced and remarried but forgot to update their 401k beneficiary might leave their retirement account to their ex-spouse despite intending it for their current spouse, and fixing this mistake after death is difficult or impossible.

Reviewing beneficiaries every few years and definitely after any marriage or divorce prevents these problems.

The statement we get quarterly or annually shows account balance, contribution history, investment allocation, and performance, and we should actually read it rather than filing it away unopened. Someone whose statement shows they're invested entirely in a money market fund earning 2% when they thought they were in stock funds needs to know this so they can fix the allocation and get back to earning appropriate returns for their age and risk tolerance. Someone whose contributions aren't showing up in their account needs to contact HR to find out why payroll deductions aren't making it to the 401k provider.

Fees matter enormously over 30-40 year time horizons because they compound against us every year, and the difference between a 401k plan with average expense ratios of 1% and one with average expense ratios of 0.1% is hundreds of thousands of dollars in final portfolio value for someone contributing consistently over a career. We can't always control the fees our employer's plan charges, but we can choose the lowest-cost options within the available menu, and we can advocate with HR for better plan options if we're stuck with expensive funds, and we can limit contributions beyond the match if the plan is truly terrible and we have access to IRA or other lower-cost alternatives.

The overall strategy for 401k accounts involves contributing at least enough to capture full employer match, increasing contributions toward the maximum as income allows, choosing between Traditional and Roth based on current versus expected future tax rates with a bias toward hedging through diversification, selecting low-cost index funds that provide broad market exposure, rebalancing at least annually, and avoiding company stock concentration and 401k loans except in genuine emergencies. Someone who follows these principles from age 30 to 65 while earning moderate income will likely accumulate $1 million or more, while someone who contributes minimally or makes poor investment choices within their plan might end up with $300,000-400,000, and that difference determines whether retirement is comfortable or marginal.

The 403b and 457 accounts follow the same basic principles as 401k with adjustments for their specific features, and someone with access to both a 401k or 403b and a 457 can contribute the maximum to both, giving them $46,000 or $61,000 in annual contribution room including catch-up contributions after 50. This creates significant advantage for government employees who can access 457 plans alongside their 403b, potentially accumulating double what private sector workers with only 401k access can save, and someone who maximizes both accounts for 30 years will build substantially larger portfolios than peers contributing to just one.

The early access feature of 457 plans makes them particularly valuable for people planning retirement before 59.5, because the money becomes available as soon as we leave government employment without penalty or special rules, while 401k and 403b money remains locked up unless we qualify for Rule of 55 or want to set up 72(t) substantially equal periodic payments. Someone retiring from government work at 53 can access their 457 immediately to fund living expenses from 53 to 59.5, then switch to IRA withdrawals after 59.5 when the penalty disappears, creating a clean bridge strategy without the complexity and inflexibility of 72(t) plans.

The 401k is powerful but limited — limited by plan options, contribution rules, and the single employer who controls it. The IRA is the account we own ourselves, with more flexibility, more investment choices, and strategies that extend well beyond simple contributions. Understanding the difference between these two tools, and when to use each, changes how much ends up in retirement at any given savings rate.

The Accounts You Own

Individual Retirement Accounts are retirement savings accounts that we open ourselves at a brokerage like Vanguard, Fidelity, or Schwab, completely separate from any employer, and they provide tax advantages similar to 401k plans but with more investment flexibility and different contribution limits. While a 401k exists only through our employer and disappears as an option when we leave the job, an IRA belongs to us personally and stays with us regardless of employment status, and we can contribute to both an IRA and a 401k in the same year if we want to save more than the 401k limit allows or if we want access to investments not available in our employer's plan.

The IRA contribution limit of $7,000 per year in 2024 is much lower than the $23,000 401k limit, but IRAs give us access to any investment available at our chosen brokerage rather than being limited to whatever our employer's plan offers, and for people without access to a 401k, the IRA is their primary tax-advantaged retirement savings vehicle. Traditional IRA and Roth IRA are the two main types, and the $7,000 limit applies across both combined, meaning we can put $7,000 in Traditional or $7,000 in Roth or split it between them, but we can't put $7,000 in each.

Traditional IRA contributions are deductible if we're not covered by a retirement plan at work, or if we are covered but our income falls below phase-out thresholds that change annually. The deduction phases out for single filers at $73,000 to $83,000 and married filers at $116,000 to $136,000 in 2024 if covered by a workplace plan, and someone above those thresholds can still contribute but gets no deduction, creating the non-deductible Traditional IRA that's mainly useful as a stepping stone to backdoor Roth conversions. Someone earning $90,000 who has a 401k at work gets no deduction for Traditional IRA contributions but can still contribute the $7,000, which then grows tax-deferred until withdrawal, though they'll need to track the non-deductible basis carefully to avoid paying tax twice on the same money.

The distinction between deductible and non-deductible contributions matters enormously at withdrawal time because deductible contributions and all growth get taxed as ordinary income, while non-deductible contributions have already been taxed and only the growth is taxable. Someone who made $40,000 in non-deductible contributions over many years and has $100,000 in their Traditional IRA has $40,000 of basis that shouldn't be taxed again when withdrawn, but proving this requires maintaining records of Form 8606 from every year they made non-deductible contributions, and many people lose track of this documentation over decades, potentially ending up paying tax on money they already paid tax on when they contributed.

Roth IRA works oppositely from Traditional by taking contributions after we've already paid tax on the money, but then letting everything grow and withdraw completely tax-free in retirement, and the contribution limit of $7,000 per year in 2024 applies across both Traditional and Roth combined, so we can't put $7,000 in each. Roth IRA contributions face income limits regardless of workplace plan coverage, phasing out at $146,000 to $161,000 for single filers and $230,000 to $240,000 for married filers in 2024. Direct contributions to Roth get made with after-tax money but grow tax-free and withdraw tax-free, and the principal can be withdrawn anytime without penalty or taxes, making Roth a useful emergency fund as well as retirement account for people who can access it.

The ability to withdraw Roth contributions anytime provides flexibility that Traditional IRA doesn't offer, because someone who contributed $7,000 annually for ten years has $70,000 of principal that's available immediately without taxes or penalties, while the earnings must wait until 59.5 or meet other exceptions to avoid penalties. This means a 45-year-old with $70,000 in Roth contributions and $30,000 in earnings can withdraw the full $70,000 of contributions anytime for any reason, though touching the $30,000 in earnings before 59.5 triggers the 10% penalty plus income tax on the earnings unless an exception applies like first-time home purchase or qualified education expenses.

Backdoor Roth mechanics work like this: contribute $7,000 to Traditional IRA with no deduction because our income is above the phase-out threshold, immediately convert that $7,000 to Roth IRA, and pay taxes on any gains between contribution and conversion which should be minimal if done quickly, like within days or weeks of the contribution. The pro-rata rule creates the main complication, stating that if we have any pre-tax IRA money anywhere in our name at the end of the year, the conversion is partially taxable based on the ratio of pre-tax to after-tax money across all our IRA accounts combined.

Someone with $93,000 in pre-tax Traditional IRA from old 401k rollovers and $7,000 in non-deductible contributions has $100,000 total IRA money, and converting $7,000 to Roth means 93% of the conversion is taxable based on the $93,000 pre-tax divided by $100,000 total, so $6,510 of the $7,000 conversion gets added to taxable income and only $490 converts tax-free. This completely defeats the purpose of backdoor Roth, turning what should be a tax-free conversion into a mostly taxable event that might push us into a higher bracket and costs thousands in unexpected taxes.

The solution to pro-rata involves rolling pre-tax IRA money into a current 401k before doing backdoor Roth, if the 401k accepts incoming rollovers, which most do. This gets the pre-tax money out of IRA accounts entirely, leaving only the non-deductible contribution that can convert to Roth tax-free, and the pro-rata calculation looks at IRA balances at year-end, so someone who rolls $93,000 from IRA to 401k in March, makes a $7,000 non-deductible IRA contribution in April, and converts it to Roth in May has zero pre-tax IRA money at year-end and the entire conversion is tax-free. Without this step, backdoor Roth doesn't work for people with pre-existing IRA money, and they're better off just keeping their money in Traditional IRA or doing Roth conversions later in retirement when they can control the tax impact.

The mechanics require careful sequencing and record-keeping because we're making a non-deductible contribution to Traditional IRA, filing Form 8606 with our taxes to document the non-deductible basis, converting that money to Roth IRA, and tracking everything to prove to the IRS that we already paid tax on the contribution so the conversion shouldn't be fully taxable. Someone who skips filing Form 8606 or loses the documentation might end up paying tax on the conversion even though they already paid tax on the contribution, creating double taxation on the same $7,000 that could have been avoided with proper paperwork.

The conversion itself happens through the brokerage where we hold the accounts, usually requiring a few clicks on their website to move money from Traditional IRA to Roth IRA, and we want to do this quickly after the contribution to minimize gains that would be taxable even in a proper backdoor conversion. Someone who contributes $7,000 and waits six months to convert might see it grow to $7,500, making the $500 gain taxable even though the $7,000 principal converts tax-free, while someone who converts within days of contributing probably has minimal gains that add negligible tax liability.

Mega backdoor Roth is a different strategy available to people whose 401k plans allow after-tax contributions beyond the regular contribution limit and either in-service conversions to Roth 401k or in-service distributions to Roth IRA. The total contribution limit across all sources including employee and employer contributions is $69,000 in 2024, or $76,500 with catch-up contributions, and someone who contributes $23,000 in regular 401k contributions and receives $6,000 in employer match has $40,000 of room remaining that could potentially be filled with after-tax contributions if the plan allows.

These after-tax contributions aren't the same as Roth contributions because they go into a separate after-tax 401k account where the principal has already been taxed but the earnings are taxable when withdrawn, creating an awkward middle ground that's less favorable than either Traditional or Roth. The magic happens when we can convert these after-tax contributions to Roth either within the 401k through an in-plan Roth conversion or by rolling them to a Roth IRA while still employed, turning the after-tax contributions into Roth money where both principal and future earnings grow and withdraw tax-free.

Someone who contributes $23,000 to regular 401k, receives $6,000 employer match, and then contributes $40,000 in after-tax contributions has put $63,000 into their 401k in a single year, and if they can convert that $40,000 in after-tax contributions to Roth 401k immediately, they've essentially made a $40,000 Roth contribution that wouldn't normally be allowed under the $23,000 regular limit. Doing this for 30 years from age 35 to 65 puts $1,200,000 in Roth money that grows to perhaps $3.8 million at 65, and all withdrawals are tax-free forever with no required minimum distributions, creating enormous tax-free wealth that completely changes retirement planning.

Not all plans allow after-tax contributions, and many that do allow them don't permit immediate conversion to Roth, requiring the after-tax money to sit and accumulate earnings that become taxable on withdrawal, reducing the benefit substantially. We need to check our specific plan documents or ask HR whether after-tax contributions are permitted and whether in-plan Roth conversions or in-service distributions to Roth IRA are allowed, and if the answer is yes to both, mega backdoor Roth becomes one of the most powerful wealth-building strategies available to high earners who can afford to contribute beyond the regular $23,000 limit.

Spousal IRA lets a non-working spouse contribute based on the working spouse's income, providing a way to save $7,000 more per year as a couple even when only one person has earnings. The working spouse must earn enough to cover both contributions, so a couple where one earns $40,000 can contribute $7,000 to each person's IRA for $14,000 total as long as they file jointly, effectively doubling their IRA contribution room. The non-working spouse can have their own Traditional IRA or Roth IRA independent of the working spouse's accounts, and the same income limits for deductibility and Roth contributions apply based on the couple's combined income.

This matters most for couples where one person stays home to care for children or elderly parents, or where one person works part-time earning below the IRA contribution limit, because it prevents the non-earning or low-earning spouse from falling behind on retirement savings. Someone who stays home from age 30 to 40 while their spouse works and contributes

$7,000 annually to a spousal IRA accumulates $100,000 or more by age 40 with reasonable investment returns, while without spousal IRA they'd have nothing saved and would be 10 years behind on retirement accumulation, creating a gap that's nearly impossible to close later.

Inherited IRA rules changed dramatically under the SECURE Act of 2019, eliminating the stretch IRA for most beneficiaries and requiring full distribution within 10 years of the original owner's death. Someone who inherits $500,000 in Traditional IRA must withdraw it all within 10 years, potentially taking $50,000 per year that gets added to their taxable income and could push them into higher brackets, and they can't just take minimum distributions over their life expectancy like the old rules allowed. The old rule let non-spouse beneficiaries stretch withdrawals over their life expectancy, so a 50-year-old inheriting an IRA could take required minimum distributions over 34 years, paying much less tax annually and letting the money grow longer.

The new rule creates a significant tax burden for heirs who inherit large Traditional IRAs because they're forced to recognize all the taxable income within a compressed 10-year window, and someone who inherits $800,000 at age 45 while earning $100,000 annually faces impossible choices about whether to take $80,000 distributions annually for 10 years that push them into the 32% or 35% brackets, or to take uneven distributions that might reduce total tax but require careful planning. The required distributions also generate income that might affect eligibility for financial aid, healthcare subsidies, or other income-tested benefits, creating ripple effects beyond just the income tax on the distributions themselves.

Spousal beneficiaries can still roll an inherited IRA into their own IRA and treat it as their own money, taking RMDs based on their own age starting at 73 and potentially stretching distributions over 20-30 years if they're much younger than the deceased spouse. Non-spouse beneficiaries like children or siblings face the 10-year rule with no exceptions, and the only break is that if the original owner had already started taking RMDs before death, the beneficiary must take annual RMDs during the 10-year period rather than being allowed to wait until year 10 to take everything out at once.

This changes estate planning for people with large IRAs who might be better off doing Roth conversions during their lifetime to reduce what gets passed to heirs in Traditional IRA form, because Roth IRA heirs still face the 10-year distribution requirement but the distributions are tax-free, eliminating the bracket compression problem that Traditional IRA creates. Someone with $1 million in Traditional IRA at age 65 might convert $40,000-50,000 annually over 20 years while managing their own tax brackets, leaving the heirs with mostly Roth money that distributes tax-free rather than Traditional money that generates large tax bills during the mandatory 10-year distribution period.

The basis tracking for non-deductible Traditional IRA contributions follows us through rollovers, conversions, and withdrawals using Form 8606, and we're responsible for maintaining these records because the IRA custodian doesn't track basis for us. Someone who made $30,000 in non-deductible contributions spread across many years needs to maintain all those Form 8606s to prove the basis when they start taking distributions, and missing documentation can result in paying tax on money that was already taxed when contributed, creating double taxation that's hard to undo after the fact.

The aggregation rule treats all Traditional IRAs as a single account for purposes of determining what portion of any withdrawal is taxable, so someone with $70,000 in total Traditional IRA consisting of $30,000 in non-deductible contributions and $40,000 in deductible contributions plus earnings has a basis of $30,000 out of $70,000 total, meaning 43% of any withdrawal is tax-free and 57% is taxable. They can't selectively withdraw just the non-deductible portion to get tax-free distributions, and they can't treat different IRA accounts differently even if they're at different custodians, because the IRS aggregates all Traditional IRAs when determining taxation of distributions.

Roth IRA conversions are different from Roth contributions and involve moving money from Traditional IRA to Roth IRA, paying income tax on the converted amount in the year of conversion, but then having that money grow and withdraw tax-free forever after a five-year waiting period. Someone with $200,000 in Traditional IRA who converts $40,000 to Roth in a given year adds $40,000 to their taxable income that year, potentially pushing into higher brackets and increasing their tax bill by $8,000-12,000 depending on their bracket, but that $40,000 then grows tax-free and can be withdrawn tax-free in retirement without increasing taxable income or affecting Social Security taxation or Medicare IRMAA surcharges.

The strategy of doing partial Roth conversions annually in retirement before RMDs start at 73 lets us control the tax hit by filling up lower brackets each year rather than waiting until 73 when RMDs force large distributions that might push us into higher brackets. Someone who retires at 60 with $800,000 in Traditional IRA and converts $35,000 annually from 60 to 72 pays tax on $455,000 of conversions at relatively low rates while managing their brackets, and by 73 they've moved more than half their money to Roth, reducing future RMDs and the associated tax complications. This requires living on other money during the conversion years, like taxable account withdrawals or Roth IRA withdrawals of previously converted amounts, but it reduces lifetime taxes and provides more flexibility in late retirement.

The five-year rules for Roth accounts create timing complications that affect when we can access money tax and penalty-free, and there are actually two different five-year rules that apply to different situations. The first five-year rule says we must have had any Roth IRA open for at least five years before we can withdraw earnings tax-free and penalty-free, and this clock starts January 1 of the year we first contributed to any Roth IRA, so someone who opens their first Roth IRA in December 2024 with a contribution for tax year 2024 starts their five-year clock on January 1, 2024, and can withdraw earnings tax-free starting January 1, 2029 as long as they're also over 59.5.

The second five-year rule applies to Roth conversions and says that each conversion has its own five-year waiting period before the converted principal can be withdrawn penalty-free if we're under 59.5, and this clock starts January 1 of the conversion year. Someone who converts $30,000 from Traditional IRA to Roth IRA in December 2024 can't withdraw that $30,000 penalty-free until January 1, 2029 unless they're over 59.5, in which case the penalty doesn't apply anyway and the five-year rule doesn't matter. This creates the Roth conversion ladder strategy for early retirement where we convert money five years before we need it, letting each conversion season for five years before withdrawal.

The ordering rules for Roth IRA distributions determine which money comes out first when we take withdrawals, and this affects tax and penalty treatment because different types of money in the Roth have different rules. Contributions always come out first and are always tax-free and penalty-free because we already paid tax on them when we contributed, conversions come out second in the order they were converted, and earnings come out last. This means someone with $50,000 in contributions, $30,000 in conversions, and $20,000 in earnings who withdraws $60,000 takes out all $50,000 of contributions tax and penalty-free, then $10,000 of the oldest conversion which might or might not incur penalty depending on the five-year rule and their age.

Recharacterization used to allow us to undo Roth conversions or contributions by moving the money back to Traditional IRA as if the conversion or contribution never happened, but this was eliminated for conversions in 2018, and now conversions are permanent and can't be undone. We can still recharacterize Roth contributions to Traditional contributions or vice versa until the tax filing deadline including extensions, which matters if we discover after contributing that our income was too high to contribute to Roth directly, but the conversion prohibition means we can't convert money to Roth, watch it decline in value, and then recharacterize back to Traditional to avoid paying tax on the pre-decline value.

The creditor protection for IRAs varies by state but generally provides strong protection from lawsuits and bankruptcy up to about $1.5 million in total IRA assets as of 2024, with unlimited protection for money rolled over from employer plans. Someone with $800,000 in IRA from rollover plus $300,000 from direct contributions has $800,000 that's fully protected and $300,000 that's protected up to the federal limit, and state law might provide additional protection beyond the federal floor. This makes IRAs a better asset protection vehicle than taxable accounts where assets are generally available to creditors, though worse than 401k accounts which have unlimited protection under ERISA regardless of the source of the money.

Required minimum distributions from Traditional IRAs start at age 73 under current law and force us to withdraw increasing percentages each year based on IRS life expectancy tables, and failing to take RMDs results in a penalty of 25% of the amount we should have withdrawn, reduced to 10% if we correct the error within two years. Someone with $500,000 in Traditional IRA at age 73 must withdraw roughly $18,900 that year, and if they forget or miscalculate and don't take the full amount, they owe penalty on the shortfall in addition to the income tax they owe on whatever they did withdraw. Roth IRAs have no RMDs during the owner's lifetime, which is one of their major advantages over Traditional accounts.

The aggregation of RMDs works differently for different account types, where we can total up all our Traditional IRA RMDs and take the full amount from one IRA or spread it across multiple IRAs as we choose, but 401k RMDs must be calculated separately for each 401k and taken from that specific account. Someone with two Traditional IRAs and two old 401k accounts can calculate RMDs on both IRAs, add them up, and take the total from whichever IRA they prefer, but they must calculate RMD on each 401k separately and take each 401k's RMD from that specific account, creating more complexity when managing multiple old 401k accounts.

The strategic use of IRAs involves maximizing contributions throughout working years, choosing between Traditional and Roth based on current and expected future tax rates, using backdoor Roth when income exceeds direct contribution limits, considering Roth conversions in early retirement before RMDs start, maintaining proper documentation for any non-deductible contributions, and understanding the rules around withdrawals, penalties, and required distributions. Someone who manages these details well can build substantial IRA wealth that provides tax-efficient income in retirement, while someone who ignores basis tracking, misses RMDs, or withdraws at the wrong times can generate unnecessary taxes and penalties that reduce lifetime wealth significantly.

The IRA and 401k get most of the attention. The HSA gets almost none, despite having better tax treatment than either one. For people who qualify, it's the only account that gives a tax deduction going in, tax-free growth in the middle, and tax-free withdrawals at the end — if it's used correctly. Most people don't use it correctly.

The Most Overlooked Account

Health Savings Accounts pair with high-deductible health insurance plans and were originally designed to help people save for current medical expenses with tax benefits, but they actually function as superior retirement savings vehicles for people who understand the rules and can afford to pay medical costs out of pocket while employed. To qualify for an HSA, we must be enrolled in a high-deductible health plan, which the IRS defines as having a deductible of at least $1,600 for individuals or $3,200 for families in 2024, and we cannot be enrolled in Medicare, claimed as a dependent on someone else's tax return, or covered by any other health insurance that isn't high-deductible.

The contribution limits are $4,150 for individuals or $8,300 for families in 2024, with an additional $1,000 catch-up contribution available after age 55, and these limits are separate from IRA and 401k limits, meaning someone maxing out their 401k at $23,000 can also contribute $4,150 to an HSA in the same year if they have qualifying health coverage. The money goes into an HSA account at a bank or investment firm, similar to an IRA, and while some employers offer HSAs through payroll deduction like 401k contributions, we can also open and contribute to an HSA independently if we have a qualifying high-deductible plan purchased through the individual market or the ACA marketplace.

The triple tax advantage means contributions reduce our taxable income just like Traditional 401k or IRA contributions, the money grows without being taxed on dividends or capital gains like all retirement accounts, and withdrawals for qualified medical expenses come out completely tax-free, making HSA the only account that gets favorable tax treatment at all three stages. A Traditional IRA gets deduction and tax-deferred growth but pays tax on withdrawal. A Roth IRA gets tax-free growth and withdrawal but no deduction. HSA gets all three benefits if used for medical expenses, and even if used for non-medical expenses after 65 it still works like Traditional IRA with penalty-free withdrawals subject only to ordinary income tax, while using HSA money for non-medical expenses before 65 triggers both a 20% penalty and income tax on the amount withdrawn.

Using HSA for retirement rather than current medical expenses requires paying medical costs out of pocket while employed and investing the HSA money for decades of growth, letting it compound tax-free until we actually need it in retirement when healthcare costs typically escalate. Someone contributing $4,150 per year from age 30 to 65 puts in $145,250 total, and at 7% annual growth that becomes roughly $620,000 by retirement. All of that money can withdraw tax-free for medical expenses, and retirement healthcare costs between Medicare premiums, out-of-pocket expenses, dental and vision care not covered by Medicare, and potential long-term care can easily consume several hundred thousand dollars over 20-30 years of retirement, making the HSA a perfect vehicle for funding this predictable but variable expense category.

The strategy of paying current medical expenses out of pocket while letting HSA money grow requires having enough cash flow and emergency savings to cover the $3,000-8,000 annual out-of-pocket costs that typical families incur even when healthy, and someone living paycheck to paycheck or without emergency funds can't implement this approach effectively. The high-deductible plan means we're paying full price for all medical care until hitting the deductible, so a family with $5,000 in medical expenses pays that $5,000 out of pocket, and if they don't have HSA savings to draw from, they need other money to cover these costs. This creates a catch-22 where the people who most need the HSA tax benefits often can't afford the cash flow required to maximize them.

Investment options within HSA vary dramatically by provider, and many employer-selected HSA administrators have high fees and limited investment choices similar to bad 401k plans, but we're not stuck with our employer's HSA provider the way we might be stuck with their 401k. We can roll HSA money to a different provider with better investment options and lower fees anytime, moving from an employer's HSA with $50 monthly account fees and only mutual funds to a provider like Fidelity or Lively that offers free accounts and access to low-cost index funds. Someone whose employer uses an expensive HSA should open their own HSA at a better provider and roll the money over quarterly or annually, avoiding the fees that compound against us over decades.

The mechanics of HSA investing require reaching a minimum balance before investment options become available at most providers, often $1,000 or $2,000, with balances below that threshold sitting in a cash account earning minimal interest. Someone starting HSA contributions should accumulate to the minimum investment threshold as quickly as possible, then invest in the same type of low-cost index funds we'd use in IRA or 401k, choosing total stock market funds or target-date funds appropriate for a retirement timeline. The investment allocation can be more aggressive than regular retirement accounts because we're less likely to need HSA money before Medicare age when other retirement accounts might need to start funding living expenses.

The receipt-saving strategy adds another layer of flexibility by letting us reimburse ourselves for old medical expenses many years or even decades after incurring them, because HSA withdrawals don't need to happen in the same year as the medical expense as long as we have documentation proving the expense occurred after the HSA was established. Someone who pays $3,000 in medical expenses at age 35 can save the receipts and reimburse themselves at age 70, and between ages 35 and 70 that $3,000 stayed invested growing tax-free. This approach requires organized record-keeping with receipts, explanation of benefits forms, and other documentation that proves the medical expenses were real and unreimbursed, and we need to maintain these records for potentially 40+ years.

The accumulation of reimbursable expenses over a career creates a pool of tax-free withdrawal capacity that can be tapped anytime, essentially functioning as a emergency fund that's been growing tax-free for decades. Someone who incurred $80,000 in out-of-pocket medical expenses from age 30 to 60 while saving receipts has $80,000 that can be withdrawn from their HSA tax-free for any purpose by claiming it's reimbursement for those old expenses, and this $80,000 might have grown to $250,000 by age 60 through investment returns, giving them the choice of either taking $80,000 tax-free through reimbursement or leaving the money to continue growing for actual medical expenses in retirement.

The risk of the receipt-saving strategy is that we might lose documentation over decades, or that IRS rules might change to disallow reimbursements beyond some time limit, or that the receipts might not meet documentation requirements if audited. Someone who claimed reimbursement for medical expenses from 30 years ago would need to produce receipts, credit card statements, insurance explanation of benefits, and other proof that the expenses were legitimate and unreimbursed, and if they can't produce adequate documentation, the withdrawal gets treated as taxable income plus the 20% penalty if they're under 65. The safeguard is keeping digital copies of all documentation with multiple backups and maintaining organized files that we can access decades later.

Qualified medical expenses that can be withdrawn tax-free from HSA include obvious things like doctor visits, hospital stays, prescription medications, and dental and vision care, but also many less obvious expenses like over-the-counter medications with a prescription, medical equipment like wheelchairs and hearing aids, long-term care services, and insurance premiums for Medicare Part B and Part D but not Medigap or Medicare Advantage premiums. The list of qualified expenses is extensive and covers most things related to diagnosing, treating, or preventing disease, but it doesn't cover cosmetic procedures, vitamins and supplements unless prescribed for specific conditions, or general health items like gym memberships and regular food regardless of how healthy.

Using HSA money for Medicare premiums provides valuable flexibility in retirement because Part B and Part D premiums can be paid from HSA tax-free, reducing the burden of increasing Medicare costs as IRMAA surcharges kick in for higher earners or as base premiums increase over time. Someone paying $500 per month for Medicare including Part B, Part D, and potentially IRMAA surcharges can use $6,000 annually from HSA to cover these premiums tax-free, and over 20 years of retirement this might total $120,000-150,000 as premiums increase with inflation and income-related adjustments, consuming a significant portion of accumulated HSA balance while avoiding taxes on those withdrawals.

The prohibition on HSA contributions once we enroll in Medicare creates a planning consideration around when to sign up for Medicare versus continuing to work and contribute to HSA. Someone who turns 65 while still working and covered by employer health insurance might delay Medicare enrollment to continue HSA contributions, accumulating another $5,150 including catch-up contributions for each year they delay Medicare. Working until 68 instead of 65 adds three more years of contributions totaling $15,450 plus growth, but it also means three more years without Medicare coverage and potentially higher out-of-pocket costs under employer health insurance, and we need to weigh these trade-offs based on our specific situation.

The automatic enrollment in Medicare Part A when we claim Social Security creates problems for HSA contributions because once we're enrolled in any part of Medicare we can no longer contribute to HSA, and the Part A enrollment happens retroactively for six months when we sign up, creating potential excess contribution penalties if we didn't know we were enrolled and kept contributing during those six months. Someone who turns 65 in January and claims Social Security in July gets enrolled in Part A effective the prior January, meaning any HSA contributions from January through July are excess contributions subject to 6% penalty unless removed before filing taxes. The solution is to either delay Social Security claiming until we're done contributing to HSA, or to stop HSA contributions six months before claiming Social Security to avoid the retroactive enrollment problem.

Long-term care insurance premiums can be paid from HSA tax-free up to certain age-based limits that range from $470 for someone under 40 to $5,880 for someone over 70 in 2024, and these limits apply per person, so a couple can potentially use $11,760 from their HSA to pay for long-term care insurance without taxes. This creates another use for accumulated HSA balances in retirement where we're paying for insurance that covers potential future catastrophic care costs using money that's been growing tax-free for decades, and the long-term care premiums we pay from HSA reduce our taxable income if we itemize medical deductions while also drawing down the HSA balance that would otherwise face taxes if used for non-medical purposes.

The interaction between HSA and other retirement accounts creates opportunities for tax-efficient retirement income planning because HSA withdrawals for medical expenses don't count as taxable income and don't affect AGI or MAGI, meaning they don't impact Social Security taxation, Medicare IRMAA surcharges, or ACA subsidy eligibility for people retiring before 65. Someone who needs $50,000 to live on and has $15,000 in medical expenses can withdraw $15,000 from HSA tax-free and $35,000 from other accounts, showing only $35,000 of income rather than $50,000, potentially keeping them under various income thresholds that trigger higher taxes or reduced benefits.

The estate planning for HSA depends on beneficiary designation, and naming a spouse as beneficiary lets the HSA transfer to them and become their HSA with all the same tax advantages continuing, while naming anyone else as beneficiary causes the HSA to lose its tax-advantaged status and become taxable income to the beneficiary in the year of death. Someone with $200,000 in HSA who dies and leaves it to their non-spouse children sees that $200,000 added to the children's income in the year of death, potentially pushing them into high tax brackets and generating $50,000-70,000 in federal and state taxes, while leaving it to a spouse preserves the tax advantages and lets the spouse continue using it for tax-free medical expenses.

The strategy of using HSA as a retirement account works best for people who can afford high-deductible health insurance and have the cash flow to pay current medical expenses while letting HSA money grow, typically meaning people in good health with adequate income and emergency savings. Someone with chronic conditions requiring expensive medications and frequent specialist visits might not benefit from high-deductible coverage even with HSA tax benefits, because they'll hit their deductible early in the year anyway and the total out-of-pocket costs under high-deductible plan might exceed what they'd pay under traditional plan with lower deductible and higher premiums.

The breakeven calculation between high-deductible plan with HSA versus traditional plan with no HSA depends on expected medical expenses, premium differences between the plans, employer HSA contributions if any, and our tax bracket. Someone in the 24% bracket who saves $2,000 annually in premiums by choosing high-deductible plan and contributes $4,000 to HSA saves $960 in taxes on the contribution, and if they receive $1,000 in employer HSA contributions, their total benefit is $3,960 before accounting for investment growth. If their medical expenses are $3,000 annually, they come out ahead by $960 plus growth, while if medical expenses are $6,000 they come out behind by $2,040 before considering the tax-free growth of HSA money.

The multi-decade time horizon for HSA as retirement account means small annual contribution differences compound into large ending balances, and someone contributing $4,150 annually for 30 years versus $3,000 annually accumulates $460,000 versus $330,000 at 7% growth, a difference of $130,000 from just $1,150 more per year. This argues for maximizing HSA contributions when we have access to qualifying high-deductible plans, treating it as the most tax-efficient retirement account we can access rather than just as a way to pay for current medical expenses.

The coordination with flexible spending accounts creates complexity because we can't contribute to both HSA and healthcare FSA in the same year with full amounts, though we can have a limited-purpose FSA for dental and vision expenses while also contributing to HSA. Someone whose employer offers both should generally choose HSA over FSA for the long-term tax benefits and the ability to roll balances forward indefinitely, while FSA requires using the money within the plan year or losing it under use-it-or-lose-it rules. The exception is someone with predictable large medical expenses coming in a specific year who can benefit from FSA's higher contribution limit of $3,200 in 2024 and the ability to access the full annual amount on day one of the plan year rather than waiting to accumulate contributions.

The overall strategy for HSA as retirement account involves enrolling in qualifying high-deductible health insurance, contributing the maximum annual amount while we're eligible, investing contributions in low-cost index funds rather than leaving them in cash, paying current medical expenses out of pocket while saving receipts if we want reimbursement flexibility, letting the money grow tax-free for decades, and then using it for Medicare premiums and out-of-pocket medical costs in retirement when healthcare expenses increase. Someone who executes this strategy from age 30 to 65 and then uses the HSA to fund medical costs from 65 to 90 can potentially save $50,000-100,000 in lifetime taxes compared to funding the same medical expenses from taxable accounts or Traditional retirement accounts.

The awareness of HSA as retirement account remains low despite the superior tax treatment, and many people treat it as just a way to pay for current medical expenses or don't enroll in high-deductible plans specifically to avoid HSA complexity and the cash flow burden of paying full price for medical care until hitting the deductible. Someone who misses 30 years of HSA contributions because they chose traditional health insurance for slightly lower out-of-pocket costs might give up $400,000-500,000 in tax-advantaged retirement savings, and this trade-off deserves careful consideration rather than defaulting to traditional coverage because that's what we've always had or what seems simpler.

The final consideration is that HSA remains available only while we have qualifying coverage, meaning job loss, employer plan changes, Medicare enrollment, or inability to afford high-deductible premiums can end our ability to contribute, and we should maximize contributions during the years we have access rather than assuming we'll always be able to catch up later. Someone with HSA access from age 35 to 55 through employer coverage who loses access at 55 when switching jobs to an employer without high-deductible options has missed their window for contributions from 55 to 65, losing 10 years of potential accumulation that can't be recovered later.

Retirement accounts cover the tax-advantaged saving. But they have limits — on contributions, on access before 59.5, and on investment options. The taxable brokerage account fills the gaps. For anyone planning to retire before traditional retirement age, it's not optional. It's the bridge.

The Money Outside the System

Taxable brokerage accounts become necessary when we've maxed retirement accounts, or when we're planning early retirement and need money accessible before 59.5 without penalty, or when we're high earners who can't access Roth IRA and have more to save than 401k limits allow. The lack of tax advantages gets offset by complete flexibility: no contribution limits, no required minimum distributions, no penalties for early withdrawal, and the ability to access principal plus gains anytime for any reason without needing to justify the withdrawal or meet specific conditions.

Someone who maxes out 401k at $23,000 and IRA at $7,000 and HSA at $4,150 has contributed $34,150 in tax-advantaged accounts, and if they can save more than this, the excess goes into taxable brokerage accounts where it grows subject to annual taxes on dividends and capital gains but remains completely accessible. A couple both maxing 401k, IRA, and HSA saves $68,300 in tax-advantaged accounts, and someone earning $200,000 who can save 30% annually has $60,000 to save, meaning $60,000 minus $34,150 equals $25,850 going to taxable accounts each year, accumulating to substantial balances over a 20-30 year career.

The early retirement use case for taxable accounts involves building balances during working years that can fund living expenses from retirement until 59.5 when penalty-free access to retirement accounts begins, creating a bridge period funded by taxable money. Someone retiring at 52 with $400,000 in taxable accounts can withdraw roughly $30,000 per year for seven years until 59.5, at which point the taxable account might be depleted but retirement accounts become accessible without penalty. This requires planning the taxable account accumulation during working years with awareness that it serves as bridge funding rather than permanent retirement money, and the amount needed depends on planned retirement age and spending during the bridge period.

Tax-efficient fund selection matters more in taxable accounts than in retirement accounts because we pay taxes on dividends and capital gains annually whether we want to or not, and these taxes reduce our returns compared to what we'd earn in tax-deferred accounts. Index funds that rarely trade and generate minimal capital gains work better than actively managed funds that create annual tax bills through frequent buying and selling, and the difference compounds over decades into significant variations in after-tax returns. Someone holding an S&P 500 index fund with 0.03% expense ratio and minimal turnover might pay tax on 1.5% of their account value annually from qualified dividends, while someone in an actively managed fund with 1% expense ratio and high turnover might pay tax on 3-4% of their account value from a combination of ordinary dividends and short-term capital gains.

The tax cost of 1.5% versus 3.5% on a $300,000 account in the 24% bracket means $1,080 versus $2,520 in annual taxes, a difference of $1,440 per year that compounds over 20 years into roughly $70,000 less wealth in the actively managed fund scenario. This tax drag exists on top of the higher expense ratios that actively managed funds charge, creating double punishment of higher fees and higher taxes that make active management in taxable accounts particularly unwise compared to the same approach in tax-deferred retirement accounts where only the fees matter.

ETFs provide better tax efficiency than mutual funds because of how they handle redemptions through the in-kind transfer mechanism that lets them avoid realizing capital gains when investors sell, and this structural advantage means two funds tracking the same index might generate different tax bills depending on whether they're structured as ETF or mutual fund. Someone holding Vanguard Total Stock Market ETF versus Vanguard Total Stock Market mutual fund gets nearly identical performance, but the ETF structure tends to generate slightly fewer capital gains distributions, saving perhaps $100-300 annually on a $300,000 position, and while this seems small, it compounds over decades and represents money that stays invested rather than going to taxes.

Municipal bonds provide tax-free interest for federal taxes and sometimes state taxes if we buy bonds issued by our home state, making them attractive for taxable accounts when we're in high tax brackets, though the yields are lower than taxable bonds to account for the tax advantage. Someone in the 32% federal bracket comparing a municipal bond yielding 3% versus a corporate bond yielding 4.5% needs to calculate the tax-equivalent yield: the 3% municipal bond is equivalent to a 4.4% taxable bond for someone in the 32% bracket because they'd pay 32% tax on the corporate bond interest, leaving only 3.06% after tax. The municipal bond wins by a small margin in this scenario, though someone in the 24% bracket sees the same 3% municipal bond equivalent to only 3.95% taxable, making the 4.5% corporate bond clearly better even after taxes.

The state tax exemption for in-state municipal bonds adds value for residents of high-tax states like California or New York where state income tax might be 6-13%, and a California resident in the 9% state bracket and 32% federal bracket sees a California municipal bond yielding 3% equivalent to a 5.2% taxable bond because they avoid both federal and state tax on the interest. Someone in the same brackets living in Texas with no state income tax only gets federal exemption, making the same 3% municipal bond equivalent to 4.4% taxable, demonstrating how the value of municipal bonds varies by state residency and making them more attractive for high-tax state residents.

Tax loss harvesting turns market declines into tax savings by selling losing positions to realize the loss, which can offset capital gains elsewhere or deduct up to $3,000 against ordinary income annually with unlimited carryforward of excess losses. Someone who buys $10,000 of stock that drops to $7,000 can sell at the loss, immediately buy a similar but not identical security to maintain market exposure, and use the $3,000 loss to reduce taxable income this year, saving perhaps $720 in the 24% bracket. If they have no gains to offset and losses exceeding $3,000, they can deduct $3,000 this year and carry forward the remainder to future years, potentially offsetting gains when they eventually sell appreciated positions or continuing to deduct $3,000 annually until the losses are exhausted.

The wash sale rule prevents selling a security at a loss and buying the identical security within 30 days before or after the sale, but switching between substantially similar securities works fine and lets us maintain market exposure while harvesting the loss. Selling Vanguard Total Stock Market ETF at a loss and immediately buying Schwab Total Stock Market ETF accomplishes the tax loss harvest because they're similar but not identical, and we can switch back after 30 days if we prefer the Vanguard fund. Someone who sells at a loss and repurchases the same security within 30 days has their loss disallowed and added to the cost basis of the repurchased shares, meaning they don't get the current tax benefit and instead push it into the future when they eventually sell the repurchased position.

The substantially identical standard gets murky when comparing index funds tracking the same index but offered by different companies, and the IRS hasn't provided clear guidance on whether selling Vanguard S&P 500 fund and buying Fidelity S&P 500 fund triggers wash sale rules. The conservative approach treats funds tracking the same index as substantially identical and waits 30 days or switches to a different index like total market instead of S&P 500, while the aggressive approach considers different companies' funds to be different securities even if tracking the same index. Someone who wants certainty should use genuinely different indices for tax loss harvesting, like selling total market and buying S&P 500, or selling large cap and buying mid cap, creating clear differentiation that avoids any wash sale concerns.

Asset location means putting different asset types in the most tax-efficient account types for each asset class, placing bonds and REITs that generate ordinary income in Traditional IRA where that income isn't taxed annually, while keeping stocks that generate qualified dividends and long-term capital gains in taxable accounts where they get preferential treatment. This requires having both tax-deferred and taxable accounts plus enough assets to make the location strategy meaningful, but someone with $500,000 in Traditional IRA and $300,000 in taxable can optimize by holding all bonds in the IRA and all stocks in taxable, assuming their target allocation is something like 60% stocks and 40% bonds.

The math shows why this helps: bonds generating 3% interest create $15,000 of income on $500,000, and in Traditional IRA this income accumulates tax-free until withdrawal, while in taxable accounts it would create $3,600 in annual taxes for someone in the 24% bracket. Stocks generating 1.5% qualified dividends on $300,000 create $4,500 in dividend income that's taxed at 15% preferential rate in taxable accounts for $675 in taxes, while if held in Traditional IRA the same dividends would eventually be taxed at ordinary income rates when withdrawn. The total tax on this arrangement is $675 annually from stock dividends, versus $4,275 if we held stocks in IRA and bonds in taxable, a difference of $3,600 per year that compounds to over $200,000 over 30 years.

The complication of asset location is that it requires coordinating across multiple accounts and thinking of the entire portfolio as one unit rather than managing each account separately, and it becomes harder to maintain as we accumulate accounts across multiple providers and retirement plan types. Someone with two 401k accounts from current and previous employers, two IRAs at different brokerages, an HSA, and a taxable account at yet another brokerage needs to either consolidate accounts or maintain detailed spreadsheets tracking total allocation across all accounts to ensure they're properly located. The effort is worth it for large portfolios where the tax savings reach thousands or tens of thousands annually, but someone with $100,000 total might reasonably skip the complexity for the minimal benefit.

International stocks create additional location complexity because they pay foreign dividends that sometimes have foreign taxes withheld, and these foreign taxes can be claimed as a credit against U.S. taxes when the international stocks are held in taxable accounts but the credit is lost when held in tax-deferred accounts. Someone holding $100,000 in international stock fund in taxable account might have $500 in foreign taxes withheld on dividends, and they can claim this $500 as a foreign tax credit against their U.S. tax liability, while the same position held in Traditional IRA gets the $500 withheld with no ability to claim the credit. This argues for holding international stocks in taxable accounts when possible, though the benefit is small enough that it shouldn't override other location considerations for most people.

Minimizing tax drag involves holding investments long enough to qualify for long-term capital gains treatment, which requires owning the security for more than one year, because short-term gains get taxed as ordinary income at rates up to 37% while long-term gains top out at 20% for high earners and

15% for most people. Someone in the 24% bracket who sells after 11 months pays 24% on gains, but waiting one more month drops the rate to 15%, saving 9% on every dollar of gain. The difference on a $50,000 gain is $4,500 in tax savings just for waiting a month, which makes patience valuable in taxable accounts and argues against frequent trading that constantly realizes short-term gains.

The 0% long-term capital gains bracket for people with taxable income below roughly $47,000 for singles or $94,000 for married couples in 2024 creates opportunities to realize gains tax-free by strategically selling appreciated positions in years when our income is low, like early retirement before claiming Social Security when we might have minimal taxable income. Someone who retires at 60 with $600,000 in taxable accounts showing $300,000 in unrealized gains can sell portions each year while keeping total taxable income below the 0% capital gains threshold, recognizing maybe $40,000 in gains annually without paying any federal tax on them, and this harvest-and-repurchase strategy resets the cost basis higher so future gains are smaller.

The step-up in basis at death means appreciated assets held until death get their cost basis reset to fair market value on the date of death, eliminating all the accumulated capital gains for heirs who inherit the assets. Someone who bought stock for $10,000 that's now worth $100,000 has $90,000 in unrealized gains, and if they sell before death they pay perhaps $13,500 in capital gains tax at 15%, but if they hold until death their heirs receive the stock with a basis of $100,000 and can sell immediately with no tax liability. This creates incentive to hold appreciated positions in taxable accounts until death when we have heirs who will inherit, though we need to balance this against concentration risk from holding too much of our wealth in single positions and against our own need for diversification and cash flow.

Qualified dividends get taxed at the preferential long-term capital gains rates of 0%, 15%, or 20% depending on income, while non-qualified ordinary dividends get taxed at ordinary income rates like wages and interest. Most dividends from U.S. corporations and many foreign corporations are qualified if we hold the stock for more than 60 days around the ex-dividend date, but REITs, master limited partnerships, and some foreign stocks pay non-qualified dividends that get taxed at higher rates. Someone receiving $10,000 in qualified dividends in the 24% bracket pays $1,500 at the 15% preferential rate, while $10,000 in non-qualified dividends would cost $2,400, making the distinction worth understanding when choosing investments for taxable accounts.

The specific identification of shares for sale lets us choose which tax lot to sell when we have multiple purchases of the same security at different prices, and this can minimize taxes by selling the highest cost basis shares first or maximize losses by selling the lowest cost basis shares when we want to harvest losses. Someone who bought 100 shares for $50, 100 shares for $60, and 100 shares for $70, and wants to sell 100 shares now worth $80 each can specify selling the $70 shares with only $10 per share gain, or can specify selling the $50 shares with $30 per share gain if they want to realize more gains to offset losses elsewhere. Without specific identification, the broker uses default methods like first-in-first-out or average cost that might not optimize our tax situation.

Capital gains harvesting in low-income years complements tax loss harvesting in normal years, and the combination lets us manage the size and timing of our taxable income to minimize lifetime taxes. Someone retiring at 55 with $800,000 in taxable accounts and minimal other income can harvest $40,000-80,000 in capital gains annually from 55 to 70 while staying in the 0% or 15% capital gains brackets, selling appreciated positions and immediately repurchasing them to reset basis higher, then when they claim Social Security at 70 and start RMDs at 73 they have much less in unrealized gains and lower future tax liability from the taxable account.

The estimated tax payment requirements for people with significant investment income mean we need to pay quarterly estimated taxes if we'll owe more than $1,000 when filing our return, and failing to pay enough through withholding or estimates triggers underpayment penalties. Someone who sells $200,000 of stock with $80,000 in long-term gains owes roughly $12,000 in federal capital gains tax, and if this sale happens in March they should make estimated tax payments in April, June, September, and January covering this liability rather than waiting until April of the following year when they file their return. The penalty for underpayment is relatively small, currently around 8% annually on the underpaid amount, but it's easily avoided by making timely estimated payments or adjusting withholding from other income sources.

The bunching of capital gains in specific years for large transactions like selling a business or real estate creates spiky income that pushes us into high brackets temporarily, and we can sometimes smooth this through installment sales where the buyer pays over multiple years, spreading the gain recognition across several tax years instead of one. Someone selling a business for $500,000 with $300,000 in gains faces $45,000-60,000 in capital gains tax if recognized in one year, but structuring it as $100,000 down payment and $100,000 annually for four years spreads the $300,000 gain into $60,000 per year, potentially keeping each year's gain in the 15% bracket instead of pushing into the 20% bracket with net investment income tax on top.

Dividend reinvestment in taxable accounts creates additional tax lots every time dividends get reinvested to buy more shares, and someone who holds a stock for 20 years with quarterly dividend reinvestment has 80 different tax lots to track at different cost bases. This makes record-keeping complicated and requires maintaining detailed information about every reinvestment, though modern brokers handle this automatically and provide cost basis reporting to the IRS. The alternative of taking dividends in cash rather than reinvesting simplifies tracking but means we need to manually reinvest the cash into our desired allocation, and it creates the temptation to spend the dividends rather than reinvesting them for growth.

The net investment income tax adds 3.8% on top of regular capital gains tax for high earners with modified adjusted gross income above $200,000 single or $250,000 married, and this applies to dividends, capital gains, and interest income from investments. Someone in the 20% long-term capital gains bracket faces an effective 23.8% rate on gains if they're above the NIIT threshold, and someone in the 15% bracket faces 18.8%, making tax planning around the NIIT threshold worthwhile for people whose income fluctuates near these levels. Realizing gains in years when income is below the threshold saves the 3.8% surcharge, and deferring gains to future years when we expect to be above the threshold anyway at least doesn't make things worse.

The overall strategy for taxable accounts involves choosing tax-efficient investments like index ETFs with minimal turnover, holding investments long enough to qualify for long-term capital gains treatment, harvesting losses when opportunities arise to offset gains or deduct against ordinary income, locating tax-inefficient assets like bonds and REITs in tax-deferred accounts when possible, harvesting gains in low-income years when we can use the 0% capital gains bracket, and holding appreciated positions until death to get step-up in basis when we have heirs who will inherit. Someone who implements these strategies consistently over 30-40 years can save $100,000-300,000 in lifetime taxes compared to someone who ignores tax efficiency and treats taxable accounts the same as retirement accounts.

The awareness that every transaction in taxable accounts creates potential tax consequences should influence our trading behavior and portfolio management, making us more intentional about when we sell, what we sell, and how we reinvest the proceeds. Someone who rebalances monthly and trades frequently in their taxable account generates constant tax bills from short-term gains and loss of long-term holding periods, while someone who rebalances annually or only when allocations drift significantly from targets minimizes trading and preserves long-term holding periods for preferential tax treatment. The optimal frequency depends on account size and how far allocations have drifted, but the default should be less frequent trading rather than more in taxable accounts.

Investment account returns get most of the attention in retirement planning conversations. But a consistent difference of 1% per year in fees produces larger differences in lifetime wealth than most people realize. Getting the account strategy right and then paying too much for it is like running hard while someone holds the other end of the rope.

The Hidden Percentage

Expense ratios get charged annually as a percentage of assets under management, and the difference between 1% and 0.1% looks small on paper but compounds dramatically over decades into six-figure variations in final portfolio value. Starting with $100,000 earning 7% gross returns, a 1% fee leaves us with 6% net and we have $574,000 after 30 years. The same $100,000 at 0.1% fee nets 6.9% and grows to $697,000, a difference of $123,000 just from fees on the initial $100,000. When we're adding $10,000 per year for 30 years and then withdrawing for another 30 years, the fee impact on lifetime wealth can exceed $500,000, representing years of working that get consumed by fees rather than funding our retirement.

The math works because we pay the fee every year on the entire balance, not just on gains, so even in years when the market goes nowhere or drops, we still hand over 1% of our total to the fund company. Someone with $500,000 in a fund charging 1% pays $5,000 that year in fees, and that $5,000 never gets the chance to compound over the remaining decades. The fund earning 7% before fees only keeps 6% for us, and over 40 years that gap between 6% and 7% represents tens of thousands of dollars per $100,000 invested, because the lost 1% each year doesn't just disappear but rather gets multiplied by all the years of compound growth that never happens.

Someone investing $500,000 at age 30 that grows to $7,600,000 by age 70 at 7% would only grow to $4,800,000 at 6%, a difference of $2,800,000 from that single percentage point of annual fees. This isn't an exaggeration or theoretical exercise but the actual mathematical result of compounding over 40 years, and it demonstrates why fees matter more than almost any other single factor in long-term investing success. We can't control market returns, we can't predict which stocks will outperform, but we can absolutely control what we pay in fees, and the difference between high fees and low fees is the difference between comfortable retirement and marginal retirement for many people.

Active management promises to beat the market enough to justify higher fees, but data shows that 80-90% of actively managed funds underperform their benchmark over 15-year periods, and the ones that do outperform often don't repeat their success in subsequent periods, meaning we can't reliably identify winners in advance. We're paying extra for active management that delivers worse results than passive index funds most of the time, and even when active funds do beat the index before fees, the fees often consume enough of the excess return to leave us worse off than if we'd just bought the index. A fund that beats the market by 0.5% before fees but charges 1% in fees versus a 0.1% index fund leaves us 0.6% behind annually, and over 30 years this gap compounds into hundreds of thousands of dollars on a moderate portfolio.

The challenge of picking winning active funds means that even if some active managers genuinely have skill, we can't identify them reliably before the fact, and the managers with good track records attract so much money that they can't deploy it as effectively as when they were smaller, often leading to performance degradation as the fund grows. Someone who identifies a fund that beat the market by 3% annually for the past 10 years might invest just as the fund's assets balloon from $500 million to $5 billion and the manager can no longer execute their strategy effectively, turning what looked like a winner into an underperformer going forward. The safer bet is accepting market returns through index funds and paying minimal fees rather than hoping to find the 10-20% of active managers who will actually beat the market after fees.

Index funds charge 0.03% to 0.2% typically, with total market funds at places like Vanguard and Fidelity available at 0.015% to 0.05%, and these low costs reflect the simple strategy of buying all the stocks in an index and holding them rather than constantly researching companies and trading positions. Someone investing $500,000 pays $75-250 per year in fees for index funds versus $5,000 for a typical 1% actively managed fund, and that $4,750-4,925 annual difference compounds to staggering amounts over career-length time periods. The argument for active management needs to be that it consistently beats the index by enough to cover the fee differential plus provide extra return, and the evidence shows this happens rarely enough that we shouldn't count on it.

The total cost of fund ownership includes not just the stated expense ratio but also trading costs that funds incur when buying and selling securities, bid-ask spreads that eat into returns invisibly, and sometimes 12b-1 fees that mutual funds charge for marketing and distribution. These hidden costs can add another 0.1-0.3% to the total drag on returns, making a fund that appears to charge 0.8% actually cost closer to 1.1% when all the friction is accounted for. ETFs generally have lower hidden costs than mutual funds because they trade on exchanges rather than being bought directly from the fund company, and the arbitrage mechanism that keeps ETF prices in line with net asset value happens through institutional investors rather than through the fund manager trading in response to investor flows.

Advisor fees typically run 1% of assets under management for traditional financial advisors, and while this sounds reasonable as a way to get professional help, it adds up to serious money over time and combines with fund fees to create total costs that can exceed 1.5% annually. Someone with $1 million paying 1% gives the advisor $10,000 per year, and if we're retired and spending $50,000 per year, that advisor fee consumes 20% of our annual spending. Over 30 years of retirement that's $300,000 going to the advisor, and we need to honestly assess whether the advice and hand-holding are worth that much money, because $300,000 could fund an extra six years of retirement or provide a substantial inheritance to our children.

Robo-advisors charge 0.25% and provide automated rebalancing, tax-loss harvesting, and asset allocation based on our age and risk tolerance, delivering many of the benefits of human advisors at one-quarter the cost. Someone with $1 million pays $2,500 annually to a robo-advisor instead of $10,000 to a traditional advisor, saving $7,500 per year that compounds to roughly $450,000 over 30 years at 6% returns. The trade-off is losing the human relationship and the ability to call someone with questions or concerns, and some people value that relationship and behavioral coaching enough to pay the premium, while others find the automated approach sufficient and prefer keeping the extra money for themselves.

The fee-only advisor model charges hourly rates or flat fees for specific planning work rather than ongoing asset-based fees, and this can make sense for people who need occasional help with complex decisions but don't want to pay ongoing fees on their entire portfolio. Someone paying $200 per hour for five hours of planning work every few years spends $1,000 periodically instead of $10,000 annually, saving $9,000 per year that stays invested and compounds. The challenge is finding good fee-only advisors and having the discipline to implement their recommendations ourselves rather than needing ongoing oversight, but for people with basic situations who just need periodic guidance on things like Roth conversions or Social Security claiming, this approach can save hundreds of thousands over a retirement.

The conflict of interest inherent in commission-based financial product sales means we should be skeptical of anyone who sells products for commission and claims to offer unbiased advice, because they make money when we buy what they're selling and make nothing when we don't. Someone who sells whole life insurance makes a commission of 50-100% of the first year's premium, creating enormous incentive to recommend these products even when term life insurance would be better for the client. The same applies to loaded mutual funds with front-end or back-end sales charges that pay commissions to the salesperson, and to annuities with high fees and surrender charges that generate large upfront commissions. The fee-only advisor who charges directly for advice and receives no commissions from product sales has much better incentive alignment with our interests.

The expense ratio within employer 401k plans varies wildly from excellent plans with index funds under 0.1% to terrible plans with only high-fee actively managed funds charging 1% or more, and employees have no control over the plan offerings but can at least choose the lowest-cost options within what's available. Someone whose plan offers both an S&P 500 index fund at 0.05% and an actively managed large-cap fund at 0.95% should obviously choose the index fund, saving 0.9% annually on that portion of their portfolio. If the plan offers only expensive options, we should contribute enough to get employer match but probably shouldn't contribute beyond that if we have access to IRA or other lower-cost alternatives.

The total portfolio expense ratio across all our accounts matters more than the expense ratio of any single fund, and someone with $300,000 in a 401k charging 0.4% average expense ratio and $200,000 in IRA charging 0.05% has a blended expense ratio of 0.26%, which is decent though not optimal. Computing this blended rate and tracking it over time helps us understand our total fee burden and identify opportunities to reduce costs by rolling expensive 401k money to cheaper IRA options when we leave jobs or by advocating with employers for better plan options. A 0.1% reduction in blended expense ratio on $500,000 saves $500 per year, and while that sounds small, it compounds to $30,000 over 30 years and represents money we keep rather than handing to financial companies.

The sales load on loaded mutual funds comes in front-end versions that take 3-5% of our investment upfront and back-end versions that charge surrender fees if we sell within several years, and both versions represent ways for salespeople to extract commissions from our investment without providing corresponding value. Someone investing $10,000 in a fund with 5% front-end load only gets $9,500 actually invested, immediately putting them 5% behind someone who invested in a no-load index fund, and they need to outperform by 5% just to break even. The back-end load creates lock-in where we face penalties for leaving even when the fund performs poorly, and both structures should be avoided in favor of no-load funds available at discount brokers.

The breakpoint discounts on loaded funds reduce the sales charge for large purchases, so buying $100,000 might have only a 3% load instead of 5%, but this still represents $3,000 going to the salesperson rather than being invested for our benefit, and we'd be better off buying a no-load index fund and keeping the full $100,000 working for us. The fact that loaded funds offer breakpoints reveals that the loads are negotiable and not actually necessary for the fund to operate, since they can waive or reduce them for large investors, and this argues against accepting any load at all when no-load alternatives are widely available.

The 12b-1 fees that some mutual funds charge supposedly cover marketing and distribution costs but really just extract an extra 0.25-1% annually on top of the stated expense ratio, and funds that charge 12b-1 fees should be avoided in favor of funds that don't. Someone paying 0.75% in 12b-1 fees on a $200,000 investment gives up $1,500 per year for marketing that doesn't benefit them in any way, and over 30 years this totals $45,000 plus lost growth that could have funded an extra year of retirement. The 12b-1 fee often gets buried in the fund's total expense ratio, so we need to check the fund prospectus to understand what we're actually paying.

Transaction fees at brokers can add up for people who trade frequently, with typical charges ranging from $0 for ETFs and stocks at major discount brokers to $50 or more at full-service brokers who provide research and advice along with trade execution. Someone making 50 trades per year at $10 per trade pays $500 annually in transaction fees, which might not sound like much but represents money that could be invested instead of going to the broker. The move toward commission-free trading at most major brokers has largely eliminated this cost for stock and ETF investors, though mutual fund trades sometimes still carry transaction fees at certain brokers, and we should check fee schedules before establishing accounts.

The account maintenance fees that some brokers and fund companies charge can range from $0 at discount brokers to $50-100 per year at traditional banks and brokerage firms, and these fees are completely avoidable by moving to modern discount brokers like Vanguard, Fidelity, or Schwab that don't charge account fees. Someone with four old accounts at different traditional brokers paying $75 each annually wastes $300 per year or $9,000 over 30 years that serves no purpose except enriching the broker, and consolidating to a single low-cost provider eliminates this waste.

The opportunity cost of fees is the investment returns we don't earn on the money that goes to fees instead of staying in our account, and this opportunity cost often exceeds the direct cost of the fees themselves because of compounding over many years. Someone who pays $5,000 in fees this year doesn't just lose $5,000 but loses the $40,000 or more that the $5,000 would have grown to over 30 years at 7% returns. The true lifetime cost of paying 1% instead of 0.1% on a $500,000 portfolio over 30 years of accumulation plus 30 years of withdrawal might exceed $1 million when we account for all the compound growth that never happens on the money paid in fees.

The fee disclosure requirements for 401k plans mandate that participants receive annual statements showing the fees they paid and how those fees affected their account balance, and we should actually read these disclosures rather than filing them away unopened. Someone whose fee disclosure shows they paid $3,000 in fees last year on a $300,000 balance knows they're paying 1% annually and should investigate whether better options exist within the plan or whether they should limit contributions beyond the employer match. The disclosure also helps compare costs across different plan options if we're choosing between jobs or evaluating whether to roll old 401k money to IRA.

The all-in cost of retirement investing for someone using low-cost index funds in IRA and 401k should be under 0.15% annually once we account for expense ratios and any small administrative fees, meaning someone with $500,000 pays under $750 per year for investment management. Adding a robo-advisor brings total cost to maybe 0.35% or $1,750 annually, while traditional advisor plus average mutual fund fees might total 1.5% or $7,500 annually on the same portfolio. The difference of $5,750 per year compounds to $350,000 over 30 years, representing a huge portion of total portfolio value that gets diverted to fees rather than funding retirement.

The strategy for minimizing fees involves choosing low-cost index funds over actively managed funds, avoiding loaded funds with sales charges, using discount brokers that don't charge account fees or transaction fees, limiting or eliminating use of traditional advisors who charge asset-based fees, being aware of hidden costs like 12b-1 fees and trading costs, and periodically reviewing total portfolio costs to identify reduction opportunities. Someone who implements this strategy from age 25 to 75 can save $500,000-1,000,000 in lifetime fees compared to someone who accepts industry-average fees, and this savings translates directly into additional retirement security or earlier retirement dates.

The psychological resistance to fee minimization often stems from the desire for professional help and the belief that higher fees must deliver higher returns, but the evidence consistently shows that lower fees predict better outcomes more reliably than any other measurable factor, and the cheapest index funds beat the majority of expensive actively managed funds over long periods. Someone who overcomes the emotional pull toward active management and expensive advisors in favor of boring low-cost index funds makes one of the best financial decisions possible, even though it feels anticlimactic and doesn't provide the narrative satisfaction of finding the hot fund manager who beats the market.

The compounding effect of fee savings means that small differences in annual costs become enormous differences in final wealth over career-length time periods, and someone who starts paying attention to fees at age 30 instead of age 50 captures an extra 20 years of compound growth on the fee savings, potentially adding $200,000-400,000 to final portfolio value. The earlier we minimize fees, the more dramatic the impact, and someone in their 20s or 30s who chooses low-cost index funds over typical actively managed funds might retire years earlier or with substantially higher standard of living from this single decision.

Once we've minimized fees, the next question is how to allocate what's inside those accounts — how much in stocks, how much in bonds, and how to think about that split as retirement approaches. The conventional rules are useful starting points. They also break down in ways worth knowing before the portfolio gets tested.

How Much Risk You Can Handle

The age-based rule of thumb suggests holding 100 minus our age in stocks, so someone who is 40 holds 60% stocks and 40% bonds, shifting toward bonds as we get older to reduce volatility as we approach and enter retirement. The newer version uses 120 minus age to account for longer lifespans and better historical market performance, giving that same 40-year-old an 80% stock allocation instead of 60%. Both versions oversimplify a decision that depends on risk tolerance, time horizon, other income sources, and personal circumstances that can't be captured in a simple formula, and someone at 40 with a pension coming at 65 can take more equity risk than someone at 40 with no pension who must fund retirement entirely through personal savings.

The fundamental trade-off is that stocks provide higher expected returns over long periods but with much higher volatility and the possibility of significant losses in any given year or even multi-year period, while bonds provide stability and steady income but lower long-term returns that might not keep pace with inflation over retirement. Someone who is 30 and won't touch their money for 35 years can tolerate stock market crashes because they have time to recover and continue buying during downturns, while someone who is 65 and needs to start withdrawing next year can't afford a 40% portfolio drop that forces them to sell stocks at depressed prices to fund living expenses.

Risk tolerance varies enormously between individuals regardless of age, and someone who panics and sells everything during market downturns shouldn't hold high stock allocations even if they're young, because the behavioral response of selling low and buying high will destroy returns regardless of what asset allocation theory suggests. Someone who watches their $500,000 portfolio drop to $300,000 in a bear market and sells everything in panic locks in the losses and misses the recovery, turning a temporary decline into a permanent one, and this person needs enough bonds to prevent panic even if it means accepting lower long-term returns.

The right allocation is the one we can stick with through market volatility without making emotional decisions that sabotage our plan.

The time horizon for different goals creates different appropriate allocations within the same portfolio, and someone who is 50 planning to retire at 65 has 15 years for retirement money but might also have college expenses in 5 years and down payment savings for a house in 2 years. The retirement money can stay mostly in stocks because it has 15 years to recover from downturns, the college money should shift toward bonds as the expense approaches to avoid being forced to sell stocks at a bad time, and the house down payment should be entirely in cash or short-term bonds because we can't risk a 30% decline right before we need the money.

Rebalancing forces us to buy low and sell high by returning to our target allocation when market movements push us off course, creating disciplined contrarian behavior that feels uncomfortable but tends to improve returns over time. A 60% stock and 40% bond portfolio that grows to 70% stocks and 30% bonds through strong stock gains gets rebalanced by selling some stocks and buying bonds, locking in some of the stock gains before a potential reversal and positioning us to benefit when bonds outperform or when stocks decline and we can shift back the other direction. The calendar approach rebalances quarterly or annually regardless of how far off target we've drifted, while the threshold approach waits until we're 5% or more away from target before rebalancing.

The calendar method has the advantage of simplicity and creates regular discipline without requiring monitoring, but it might trigger unnecessary trading and taxes in years when allocations haven't drifted much from target. Someone rebalancing annually who checks their portfolio on January 1st and finds they're 61% stocks instead of 60% probably shouldn't bother rebalancing for a 1% drift, while someone who is 68% stocks is meaningfully off target and should rebalance. The threshold method only acts when drift is significant but requires more monitoring to know when thresholds are hit, and in taxable accounts where rebalancing triggers capital gains taxes, we probably want higher thresholds like 10% drift before acting.

Risk management shifts from accumulation to distribution when we retire because we can no longer replace losses through additional contributions and we're withdrawing money regardless of market conditions, creating sequence of returns risk that doesn't exist while working. Someone working and adding $20,000 per year to their portfolio can ride out a 30% decline knowing their contributions are buying at lower prices and the recovery will eventually make them whole, but someone in retirement withdrawing $40,000 per year experiences a double impact where the portfolio drops 30% and they're selling shares at depressed prices to fund living expenses, locking in losses that can never be recovered because those shares are gone.

The bond tent strategy increases bond allocation for five years before retirement and five years after, creating a tent shape where bonds peak around the retirement date then decline back toward more stocks once we've survived the dangerous early retirement period when sequence risk is highest. Someone retiring at 60 might hold 50% bonds from 55 to 65, protecting against the worst sequence where a market crash right at retirement destroys the plan, then gradually shift back to 30% bonds by age 70 once the critical period has passed and they can afford to take more equity risk again with reduced portfolio size but longer remaining time horizon.

The logic of increasing stock allocation in later retirement after reducing it at retirement sounds counterintuitive but makes sense when we consider that someone who successfully navigates the first 10 years of retirement without portfolio failure has demonstrated their plan works and can afford more volatility chasing higher returns, while someone who is 65 with their full portfolio intact faces maximum risk from poor early returns. The bond tent trades some long-term return for protection during the vulnerable transition period, accepting that if markets perform well from 60-70 we'll underperform by holding extra bonds, but if markets crash we'll survive while someone who stayed at high stock allocation might fail.

International diversification provides exposure to markets outside the U.S., reducing the concentration risk of betting everything on American companies and capturing growth in other economies that might outperform the U.S. in certain periods. The U.S. market has outperformed international markets for the past decade plus, leading some people to question why they should hold international stocks at all when U.S. stocks have delivered better returns, but historical periods exist where international outperformed and home country bias makes us overweight what's familiar rather than what's optimal for diversification.

A reasonable allocation might be 30-40% of stock holdings in international funds, recognizing that we're already exposed to international economies through U.S. multinationals that generate substantial revenue overseas but wanting broader geographic diversification anyway. Someone with $600,000 in stocks might hold $400,000 in U.S. total market and $200,000 in international total market, capturing both U.S. and international returns while avoiding the concentration risk of all-domestic holdings. The exact percentage matters less than having some international exposure, and anything from 20-50% of stocks in international represents reasonable diversification.

The currency risk in international investing means that returns get affected not just by how the underlying stocks perform but also by currency exchange rate movements, and a foreign stock that gains 10% in its local currency might only return 5% to a U.S. investor if the local currency weakens against the dollar. This adds volatility that pure domestic investing avoids, but it also provides some hedge against dollar weakness where U.S. stocks might struggle but international holdings benefit from a strengthening foreign currency. Someone who holds international stocks accepts this additional volatility in exchange for broader diversification and the possibility of benefiting when non-U.S. markets outperform.

The small-cap and value tilts that some investors add to their stock allocation attempt to capture higher returns from smaller companies and from stocks trading at low valuations relative to fundamentals, based on research showing these factors have historically provided excess returns. Someone might hold 70% in total market index funds and 30% in small-cap value funds, overweighting areas of the market that theory suggests should outperform, though the empirical evidence is mixed and these tilts add complexity without guaranteed benefit. The simpler approach of just holding total market funds captures these factors through their weight in the overall market without trying to overweight them, and for most people this simplicity is worth more than the potential extra return from factor tilting.

The bond allocation within the fixed income portion can be simple or complex, with the simple version holding total bond market index funds that own everything from short-term treasuries to long-term corporate bonds in market weights, and the complex version splitting between different types and maturities based on specific objectives. Someone might hold 50% in intermediate-term treasury bonds for safety and deflation protection, 30% in TIPS for inflation protection, and 20% in short-term bonds for liquidity, creating a more tailored fixed income allocation than just buying total bond market. The complexity adds work and the benefit is debatable for most people, but someone with strong views on inflation or interest rate direction might find it worthwhile.

The role of bonds in a portfolio is primarily stability and diversification rather than return generation, and we should expect bonds to deliver lower returns than stocks over long periods in exchange for much lower volatility and the tendency to hold value or even gain when stocks decline. Someone who expects bonds to match stock returns will be disappointed and might abandon bonds at exactly the wrong time, while someone who understands bonds as portfolio ballast that reduces overall volatility and provides dry powder to rebalance into stocks during declines will appreciate their role even when they underperform stocks for extended periods.

The TIPS allocation provides inflation protection through bonds that adjust their principal value based on CPI, ensuring that the real purchasing power of the investment is maintained even if inflation accelerates. Someone holding $100,000 in TIPS sees the principal increase to $103,000 if inflation is 3%, and the coupon payments also increase because they're calculated as a percentage of the inflation-adjusted principal, providing a real return that's protected against inflation. The trade-off is that TIPS typically yield less than nominal bonds of similar maturity, so we're paying for the inflation insurance through lower baseline yields, and in periods of low inflation this insurance proves unnecessary and we would have been better off in nominal bonds.

Cash and money market funds serve as the ultimate stability in a portfolio, providing completely stable principal value and liquidity, though returns barely keep pace with inflation and sometimes fall behind, meaning cash loses purchasing power in real terms over long holding periods. Someone should hold enough cash for emergency expenses of 3-6 months of spending, and maybe an additional year or two of planned retirement expenses if they're recently retired and want extra cushion against needing to sell stocks in a downturn, but holding more cash than this in a long-term portfolio sacrifices too much growth for stability we don't actually need.

The glide path of target-date funds automatically adjusts allocation from aggressive when young to conservative when old, following a predetermined path that's based on the target retirement year in the fund name. Someone buying a 2050 target-date fund in 2024 gets maybe 90% stocks and 10% bonds initially, shifting gradually to perhaps 50% stocks and 50% bonds by 2050 and continuing to shift toward 30% stocks and 70% bonds by 2065 when the fund assumes we're fully retired. This autopilot approach removes the need for rebalancing decisions and prevents us from making emotional allocation changes during market stress, though it locks us into the fund company's assumptions about appropriate allocation which might not match our specific circumstances.

The criticism of target-date funds is that they use one-size-fits-all allocation based only on age without considering our specific risk tolerance, other income sources, portfolio size, or health status, and they often charge higher expense ratios than building the same allocation with individual index funds. Someone with a pension coming might want more stock exposure than the target-date fund provides because they have guaranteed income covering basic needs, while someone in poor health expecting a shorter retirement might want less stock exposure than a fund designed for average life expectancy. The convenience of target-date funds appeals to people who want simple autopilot investing, while people with more complex situations or who want to minimize fees might prefer building their own allocation.

Asset location coordinates with asset allocation by placing different asset classes in the most tax-efficient accounts, and someone with both taxable and tax-deferred accounts needs to think about the entire portfolio allocation while being strategic about where each asset lives. Someone targeting 60% stocks and 40% bonds with $600,000 in 401k and $400,000 in taxable should put all $400,000 of bonds in the 401k where the interest income isn't taxed annually, plus $200,000 of stocks to fill out the 401k, while the $400,000 taxable account holds stocks that generate qualified dividends taxed at preferential rates. This achieves the same 60/40 overall allocation as holding 60/40 in each account but with better tax efficiency.

The complexity of coordinating allocation across multiple accounts and account types increases with each additional account we accumulate over our careers, and someone with two 401k accounts from current and previous employers, two IRAs, an HSA, and a taxable account needs either detailed spreadsheets or portfolio aggregation software to track their total allocation and ensure it matches their target. The alternative of simplifying by consolidating accounts where possible makes the coordination easier, and someone who rolls old 401k money into IRA whenever changing jobs and maintains a single taxable account has fewer moving parts to coordinate than someone with six or eight scattered accounts.

The withdrawal location strategy in retirement coordinates with asset location by prioritizing withdrawals from taxable accounts first to preserve tax-advantaged growth in retirement accounts, though this gets modified based on specific circumstances like needing to stay under ACA subsidy thresholds or managing future RMDs. The basic sequence of taking from taxable accounts first, then Traditional retirement accounts, then Roth creates efficient use of the different account types, but someone who is 64 and wants to do Roth conversions before RMDs start at 73 might reverse this and withdraw from Traditional IRA to fund spending while doing conversions, even though this increases current taxes.

The overall strategy for asset allocation involves choosing a stock-bond mix based on age, risk tolerance, and time horizon, typically starting aggressive when young and shifting toward conservative as we approach and enter retirement, rebalancing periodically to maintain target allocations, including some international stocks for geographic diversification, using simple low-cost index funds rather than complex factor tilts or active management, and coordinating allocation across all accounts while being strategic about asset location for tax efficiency. Someone who implements this strategy consistently and resists the temptation to make dramatic changes based on market predictions or recent performance will likely achieve better results than someone who chases returns or panics during downturns.

The behavioral challenge of maintaining allocation discipline during market extremes often matters more than the specific allocation chosen, and someone who sticks with a 70-30 stock-bond mix through bull and bear markets will probably outperform someone who shifts between 100% stocks after gains and 30% stocks after declines even though the latter might seem like smart tactical moves. The emotional difficulty of buying stocks when they've fallen 30% and selling them when they've risen 50% is real, and having a predetermined allocation with mechanical rebalancing helps us do the right thing even when it feels wrong.

Asset allocation determines how the portfolio grows. Social Security determines the floor below which retirement income can't fall. And unlike portfolio returns, Social Security is guaranteed by the federal government, adjusted for inflation, and paid for as long as we're alive. Understanding how the benefit is calculated — before thinking about when to claim it — changes how we see the claiming decision.

How Social Security Is Built

Social Security calculates benefits based on the highest 35 years of earnings after adjusting for wage inflation, so someone who earned $30,000 in 1990 gets that amount indexed to current wage levels before it enters the calculation, reflecting the reality that wages generally rise over time and what seemed like good money 30 years ago would be quite modest by today's standards. The system takes the top 35 years after this indexing process, averages them to get Average Indexed Monthly Earnings, applies a progressive formula that gives higher replacement rates to lower earners, and produces a Primary Insurance Amount that represents what we'd get at full retirement age, which is 67 for people born in 1960 or later.

The indexing to wage growth rather than price inflation means that someone who earned $50,000 in 2000 doesn't just get credit for $50,000 but gets that amount multiplied by the ratio of average wages in the year they turn 60 to average wages in 2000, potentially turning the $50,000 into $75,000 or more in indexed earnings. This indexing stops at age 60, and earnings after that get counted at their actual nominal value without further adjustment, which creates a strange situation where someone who earned $80,000 at age 58 might have higher indexed earnings than if they earned $85,000 at age 62 because the $80,000 gets indexed upward but the $85,000 doesn't.

Years with zero earnings count in the 35-year average if we don't have 35 years of work history, which reduces benefits for people who took time off to raise children, went to graduate school, dealt with unemployment, or entered the workforce late. Someone who worked 25 years has 10 years of zeros in their calculation, dragging down the average and reducing the final benefit compared to someone who worked continuously for 35 years at similar wage levels. The only way to eliminate those zeros is by working more years, replacing the zero years with earning years, and each replacement year increases the average if the new earnings are higher than the lowest year currently in the calculation.

The calculation methodology means that someone who worked 35 years earning $40,000 annually and then works a 36th year earning $60,000 replaces their lowest-earning year with a higher-earning year if that $60,000 is better than the worst year currently in their top 35. If all 35 previous years were already above $60,000 indexed, the additional year doesn't help because it becomes the new lowest year and doesn't replace anything lower. This makes the marginal benefit of additional working years decrease over time for people who already have 35 solid years, though there are other reasons to keep working like accumulating more retirement savings or delaying Social Security claiming to increase the benefit percentage.

The progressive formula gives someone who averaged $2,000 per month over their 35 best years a much higher replacement rate than someone who averaged $8,000 per month, creating a system where lower earners get 50-60% of their pre-retirement earnings replaced while higher earners get only 25-35% replaced. Someone who averaged $25,000 annually might get Social Security of $1,400 per month or $16,800 annually, replacing 67% of their pre-retirement earnings, while someone who averaged $100,000 annually might get $2,800 per month or $33,600 annually, replacing only 34%. This progressivity provides a stronger safety net for people with lower lifetime earnings, but it also means that high earners need more personal savings to maintain their lifestyle since Social Security won't replace as much.

The bend points in the formula determine where the replacement rate changes, and for someone reaching age 62 in 2024, the first $1,174 of Average Indexed Monthly Earnings gets replaced at 90%, the amount from $1,175 to $7,078 gets replaced at 32%, and anything above $7,078 gets replaced at 15%. Someone with AIME of $5,000 gets 90% of the first $1,174 which is $1,057, plus 32% of the remaining $3,826 which is $1,224, for a total Primary Insurance Amount of $2,281 per month at full retirement age. These bend points get adjusted annually for wage growth, so the thresholds change every year and the exact calculation depends on when we reach 62.

Full retirement age is 67 for people born in 1960 or later, though people born between 1943 and 1959 have full retirement ages between 66 and 67 depending on their exact birth year, and this full retirement age determines both when we can claim unreduced benefits and how much reduction we face for claiming early or increase we receive for delaying. Someone born in 1958 has a full retirement age of 66 and 8 months, meaning they can claim reduced benefits starting at 62 but face reduction for the 56 months between 62 and their full retirement age, while someone born in 1962 has full retirement age of 67 and faces reduction for 60 months if claiming at 62.

The early claiming reduction is roughly 5/9 of 1% per month for the first 36 months before full retirement age, and 5/12 of 1% per month for any additional months beyond 36, creating a total reduction of 30% for claiming at 62 when full retirement age is 67. Someone entitled to $2,000 at age 67 gets only $1,400 if they claim at 62, a permanent reduction that lasts their entire life, not just until they reach 67. The reduction reflects the longer expected payment period when claiming early, spreading the same lifetime benefit over more years by reducing the monthly amount, and someone who lives to average life expectancy should receive roughly the same total dollars whether they claim at 62 or 67, though the monthly amounts differ substantially.

The delayed retirement credits provide an increase of 8% per year for delaying past full retirement age up to age 70, so someone with full retirement age of 67 who delays to 70 gets 24% more than their Primary Insurance Amount. That same person entitled to $2,000 at 67 receives $2,480 if they wait until 70, and this increase also lasts for life, providing higher monthly income in exchange for starting payments later. The credits stop accruing at 70, so there's no benefit to delaying past 70 and we should claim at 70 even if we don't need the money yet, because waiting longer just gives up payments without increasing the monthly amount.

The earnings test applies to people who claim before full retirement age while still working, reducing benefits by $1 for every $2 earned above roughly $22,320 per year in 2024 for people who haven't yet reached full retirement age in that year. Someone claiming at 62 while earning $50,000 per year loses essentially all their Social Security benefits to the earnings test because they're $27,680 over the limit and lose $13,840 in benefits, which might be all or most of what they would receive depending on their benefit amount. The withheld benefits aren't completely lost because they get factored into a recalculation at full retirement age that increases the monthly benefit slightly, but the immediate effect is that working substantial amounts while claiming early results in little or no current Social Security income.

The earnings test disappears at full retirement age, so someone who reaches 67 in July can earn unlimited amounts starting in July with no reduction in Social Security benefits, though earnings in January through June of that year still face a modified earnings test with a higher threshold of about $59,520 and reduction of $1 for every $3 over the limit. Someone working full-time until 67 loses nothing by claiming at 67 even while continuing to work, but claiming at 62 and working until 67 means five years of withheld benefits that provide minimal current income, making early claiming while still employed usually pointless unless we're earning very little.

Maximum taxable earnings set the upper limit on wages subject to Social Security tax and also the maximum amount that counts toward benefit calculation, sitting at $168,600 in 2024 and adjusted annually for wage growth. Someone earning $200,000 only pays Social Security tax on the first $168,600 and only gets credit for that amount in their benefit calculation, meaning very high earners pay a lower effective rate of Social Security tax and also see their replacement rate drop because additional earnings above the cap don't increase benefits. Someone who earned at or above the maximum for 35 years receives the maximum Social Security benefit, which is roughly $3,800 per month at full retirement age in 2024, and no amount of higher earnings can increase this because the cap limits both taxes and benefits.

Checking our Social Security statement shows our earning history and estimated benefits at different claiming ages, and we should review it annually to catch errors before they become permanent because the Social Security Administration sometimes misses or misrecords earnings, particularly for people who had multiple jobs in a year or worked for small employers with poor record-keeping. Someone who worked a side job that paid $5,000 but wasn't properly reported might have a zero for that year or only partial credit, reducing their eventual benefit if not corrected. We can request corrections by providing W-2s or tax returns showing the actual earnings, but this gets harder the longer we wait, which is why annual review makes sense rather than discovering errors decades later when documentation is lost.

The online Social Security account lets us view our statement anytime rather than waiting for the mailed version, and it shows year-by-year earnings, projected benefits at 62, 67, and 70, and estimates for disability and survivor benefits. Someone who creates an account at age 40 can track their earning record and see how projected benefits change as they accumulate more work years, and they can also see how additional earnings in future years might increase their benefit by replacing lower-earning years from earlier in their career. The projections assume we'll continue earning at recent levels until the projected claiming age, so someone currently earning $80,000 sees projections based on earning $80,000 annually until they claim, which might overestimate if they plan to retire early or underestimate if they expect raises.

The taxation of Social Security benefits adds complexity because up to 85% of benefits can be taxable depending on our other income, using a formula based on combined income which is Adjusted Gross Income plus tax-exempt interest plus half of Social Security benefits. Someone with combined income below $25,000 single or $32,000 married pays no tax on Social Security, while combined income between those amounts and $34,000 single or $44,000 married makes up to 50% taxable, and combined income above those thresholds makes up to 85% taxable. This means someone receiving $30,000 in Social Security plus $40,000 from Traditional IRA withdrawals has combined income of $55,000 which is well above the threshold, making 85% of their Social Security or $25,500 subject to income tax.

The marginal effect of the Social Security taxation formula can create situations where an extra dollar of other income causes more than a dollar of additional taxable income because it pushes more Social Security benefits into the taxable range. Someone right at the threshold where benefits start becoming taxable finds that $1,000 additional IRA withdrawal adds $1,000 to their income plus causes $850 more in Social Security to become taxable, for a total taxable income increase of $1,850, effectively creating a marginal tax rate 85% higher than their bracket would suggest. This matters for Roth conversion planning and withdrawal sequencing because we might want to avoid the zone where Social Security taxation creates these extra-high marginal rates.

Spousal benefits let a lower-earning spouse claim based on the higher-earning spouse's record rather than their own if that produces a larger benefit, receiving up to 50% of the higher earner's Primary Insurance Amount when both have reached full retirement age. A couple where one person's PIA is $2,800 and the other's is $900 can have the lower earner claim a spousal benefit of $1,400 instead of their own $900, bringing combined benefits to $4,200 while both are alive. The spousal benefit requires the higher earner to have already filed for their own benefits, and it gets reduced if the lower earner claims before their full retirement age, so someone claiming spousal benefits at 62 when entitled to $1,400 at 67 only receives about $980.

Survivor benefits work differently from spousal benefits and matter enormously for married couples because when one spouse dies, the surviving spouse gets the higher of the two benefits and the lower benefit disappears completely. If the higher earner claimed at 62 and died first, the survivor inherits that reduced benefit for potentially 20-30 years, while if the higher earner delayed to 70, the survivor gets the much larger benefit. A couple where one receives $2,480 from delaying to 70 and the other receives $1,400 from claiming at 62 sees the survivor get $2,480 after the first death, while if both claimed at 62 getting $1,735 and $980, the survivor only gets $1,735 after the first death, a difference of $745 per month or $8,940 per year for potentially decades.

This creates a strategy where the higher-earning spouse delays to 70 to maximize the survivor benefit regardless of their own life expectancy, because they're really insuring the surviving spouse's life expectancy which is likely to be longer and where the higher benefit matters most. Someone in poor health might think claiming early makes sense because they probably won't live long, but if they're married and the higher earner, delaying to 70 protects the spouse who will likely outlive them and need the larger benefit during widowhood. The lower-earning spouse can claim earlier because their benefit will be replaced by the survivor benefit anyway, so there's less reason for them to delay.

Divorced spouse benefits work like spousal benefits if the marriage lasted 10 years or longer, allowing someone to claim 50% of their ex's full retirement age benefit without the ex knowing or being affected, as long as the claiming spouse is unmarried at the time of claiming. Someone married for 11 years who divorced can claim on their ex's record at full retirement age and receive up to half of what the ex gets, while someone married for 9 years gets nothing despite nearly a decade of marriage. If married multiple times for 10+ years each, we can choose which ex-spouse's record to claim on, taking whichever provides the higher benefit, though we can only claim on one ex at a time.

Government pension offset affects people who receive pensions from jobs not covered by Social Security, like many state and local government positions or certain federal jobs, reducing their Social Security spousal or survivor benefits by two-thirds of their government pension amount. Someone receiving a $1,800 monthly government pension who would otherwise get $1,200 in spousal Social Security benefits has the Social Security reduced by $1,200 which is two-thirds of $1,800, completely eliminating the Social Security spousal benefit. This prevents people from receiving full pensions from non-covered employment plus full spousal Social Security benefits, though it seems harsh for people who earned both through different jobs over their career.

Windfall elimination provision reduces Social Security benefits for people who receive pensions from non-covered employment where they didn't pay Social Security taxes but also have some Social Security-covered employment, changing the formula to reduce the replacement rate on the first bend point from 90% to as low as 40%. Someone with substantial non-covered employment who also worked 20 years in covered employment gets less generous Social Security than someone who worked only in covered employment, because the system assumes their lower covered earnings represent their total career when they actually had substantial non-covered earnings. The reduction is capped so the WEP can't reduce the Social

Security benefit by more than half the pension from non-covered work, but it still substantially reduces benefits for affected workers.

The family maximum limits total benefits that can be paid on one worker's record to between 150% and 188% of the worker's PIA depending on the benefit amount, affecting families where multiple people claim on the same record. Someone with a PIA of $2,000 and a spouse and two minor children all claiming benefits might face a family maximum of $3,500, and each dependent benefit gets reduced proportionally to stay under this cap. This mainly affects young disabled workers with minor children or older workers who married much younger spouses with minor children, and most retirement-age couples don't encounter it because just the worker and spouse claiming doesn't usually exceed the family maximum.

Cost of living adjustments increase benefits annually based on the Consumer Price Index, though the specific index used is CPI-W which measures urban wage earners and clerical workers rather than elderly consumers who spend more on healthcare. Someone receiving $2,000 per month in 2024 might receive $2,060 in 2025 if the COLA is 3%, and these adjustments compound over time so the initial benefit amount grows substantially over 20-30 years of retirement. The COLA somewhat protects against inflation though there's debate about whether it fully captures the inflation elderly people experience since healthcare costs rise faster than general prices and the CPI-W might not reflect actual spending patterns of retirees.

The substantial earnings test for disability benefits requires having worked 5 of the last 10 years before becoming disabled for most people, though younger workers face less strict requirements because they haven't had as many years to accumulate work history. Someone who becomes disabled at 52 needs to have worked at least 5 years between 42 and 52, earning above a minimum threshold that changes annually, and someone who doesn't meet this test gets no disability benefits even if they have substantial earlier work history. This creates vulnerability for people who left the workforce for several years and then become disabled before accumulating enough recent work to re-qualify.

The earnings record correction process requires filing Form SSA-7008 and providing documentation like W-2s, tax returns, or pay stubs showing the missing or incorrect earnings, and the Social Security Administration generally accepts corrections for recent years but becomes more skeptical of changes to records from decades ago. Someone who discovers at age 60 that their earnings from age 30 weren't properly recorded faces challenges proving what they earned 30 years ago if they don't have documentation, which argues for checking the record regularly and fixing errors when they're recent rather than waiting until retirement approaches. The three-year statute of limitations on corrections gets extended in cases of fraud or employer error, but we shouldn't count on getting records corrected from many years ago without solid documentation.

Knowing how the benefit is calculated is only the beginning. The claiming decision — when to start receiving benefits — can mean the difference of hundreds of thousands of dollars over a lifetime, and it interacts with marriage, health, other income sources, and the tax code in ways that make the simple break-even calculation look naive. This is where the real strategy happens.

When to Pull the Trigger on Social Security

Break-even analysis compares claiming at different ages and calculates when the higher benefit from delaying catches up to the earlier payments from claiming sooner, and people often use this framework to decide when to claim by figuring out how long they need to live for delaying to pay off financially. Claiming at 62 versus 70 typically shows break-even around age 80-82, meaning if we live past that point we come out ahead in total cumulative dollars by delaying, but if we die before that age we would have received more total money by claiming early. This framing treats Social Security as an investment decision when it's actually longevity insurance that protects against living longer than expected and running out of other resources when we're in our 80s and 90s.

The person who claims at 62 and dies at 78 appears to have "won" by getting 16 years of payments totaling perhaps $270,000 in cumulative benefits, while someone who delayed to 70 and died at 78 only got 8 years of the higher benefit totaling maybe $238,000, coming out $32,000 behind. But the person who claims at 62 and lives to 95 gets 33 years of the reduced benefit totaling about $555,000, while the person who delayed to 70 gets 25 years of the higher benefit totaling $744,000, and by age 95 the cumulative difference strongly favors the person who delayed. More importantly, at 95 our portfolio might be depleted and inflation has eroded the purchasing power of our savings, making the difference between $1,400 and $2,480 per month the difference between adequacy and hardship when we're most vulnerable.

The break-even framing also ignores the value of insurance against uncertain longevity, because someone who doesn't know if they'll live to 75 or 95 benefits more from protection against the 95 scenario than from optimizing for the 75 scenario. Running out of money at 85 after the portfolio depletes creates genuine hardship that's difficult to solve, while dying at 78 with some unclaimed Social Security benefits represents foregone money but doesn't create crisis. The asymmetry of outcomes argues for delaying Social Security to provide maximum protection in the scenarios where we need it most, even if it means potentially leaving money on the table if we die early.

Spousal benefits allow a lower-earning spouse to claim 50% of the higher earner's full retirement age benefit instead of their own benefit if that amount is larger, bringing combined benefits up but creating strategic questions about when each spouse should claim. A couple where one person's PIA is $2,400 and the other's would be only $900 sees the lower earner claim a spousal benefit of $1,200 instead of taking their own $900, bringing combined benefits to $3,600 while both are alive. The spousal benefit only reaches the full 50% if the lower earner waits until their own full retirement age to claim, and it gets reduced if claimed earlier, falling to about 35% of the higher earner's PIA if claimed at 62.

The requirement that the higher earner must have already filed for their own benefits in order for the spouse to claim spousal benefits creates coordination challenges, because if the higher earner wants to delay to 70 to maximize their benefit, the lower earner has to wait until then to access spousal benefits, potentially leaving money on the table if they could have been claiming their own reduced benefit during those years. Someone whose own benefit at 62 is $900 could claim that amount starting at 62 while the higher-earning spouse delays to 70, then switch to the larger spousal benefit of $1,200 at 70, though the switch involves some complexity and the spousal benefit gets reduced because they claimed their own benefit before full retirement age.

Survivor benefits are often misunderstood but matter enormously for married couples because when one spouse dies, the surviving spouse gets the higher of the two benefits and the lower benefit disappears completely, cutting household Social Security income by the smaller benefit amount. If the higher earner claimed at 62 receiving $1,735 and died first, the survivor inherits that reduced benefit for potentially 20-30 more years and loses their own benefit of maybe $980, leaving them with only $1,735 per month. If the higher earner delayed to 70 receiving $2,480, the survivor gets that amount and loses their own, leaving them with $2,480 per month, a difference of $745 monthly or $8,940 annually that lasts the rest of the surviving spouse's life.

This creates the strategy where the higher-earning spouse delays to 70 to maximize the survivor benefit regardless of their own life expectancy, because they're really insuring the surviving spouse's life expectancy which is statistically likely to be longer since women typically outlive men and wives are often younger than husbands. Someone in poor health might intuitively think claiming early makes sense because they don't expect to live long enough for delaying to pay off, but if they're married and the higher earner, their claiming decision affects their spouse's income for potentially decades after their death, making delay the right choice even with poor personal health prospects.

The lower-earning spouse faces different incentives because their benefit will likely be replaced by the survivor benefit anyway when the higher earner dies, making early claiming less costly since they're not permanently locking in a reduced survivor benefit. Someone entitled to $900 at full retirement age or $630 at 62 who will eventually get a $2,480 survivor benefit loses less by claiming at 62 and taking the reduced amount for several years before switching to the survivor benefit, compared to the higher earner whose claiming decision affects the survivor benefit amount. The optimal strategy often involves the lower earner claiming somewhere between 62 and full retirement age while the higher earner delays to 70, balancing current income needs against survivor benefit maximization.

The earnings test complicates early claiming decisions because someone who claims before full retirement age while still working faces $1 reduction in benefits for every $2 earned above about $22,320 in 2024, effectively eliminating Social Security benefits for anyone earning substantial income. Someone claiming at 62 while earning $50,000 per year loses essentially all their Social Security to the earnings test, paying into the system through payroll taxes while receiving little or nothing in current benefits. The withheld benefits result in a recalculation at full retirement age that increases the monthly amount slightly to account for the months of withheld benefits, but this doesn't fully compensate for the loss of current income, making early claiming while still employed generally pointless.

The test disappears at full retirement age, so someone working full-time until 67 loses nothing by claiming at 67 while continuing to work, and they can earn unlimited amounts without any reduction in Social Security benefits. Someone working from 62 to 67 should probably not claim Social Security during those years unless their earnings are quite low, instead waiting until they stop working or reach full retirement age to start benefits. The one exception might be someone working part-time earning just above the threshold who could reduce hours slightly to stay under the limit and receive full benefits, but anyone earning $40,000 or more annually before full retirement age gets little or no Social Security and should wait to claim.

Divorced spouse benefits work like spousal benefits if the marriage lasted 10 years or longer, allowing someone to claim 50% of their ex's full retirement age benefit without the ex knowing or being affected by the claim, as long as the claiming spouse is unmarried at the time. Someone married for 11 years who divorced 15 years ago can claim on their ex-spouse's record at full retirement age even if the ex has remarried and even if they haven't spoken in years, and the ex never knows their benefit is being claimed against their record because it doesn't reduce what they receive. Someone married for 9 years and 11 months gets nothing despite nearly a decade of marriage, making the 10-year threshold absolute and creating incentives for some couples to stay married just long enough to qualify.

If married multiple times for 10+ years each, we can choose which ex-spouse's record to claim on, taking whichever provides the higher benefit based on their respective earnings histories, though we can only claim on one ex at a time and we lose the divorced spouse benefit if we remarry. Someone with two ex-spouses from 12-year marriages can claim on whichever ex had higher earnings, maximizing their benefit, while someone married three times for 8 years, 7 years, and 6 years gets nothing from any ex-spouse despite 21 years of total marriage, demonstrating how the 10-year requirement can disadvantage people with multiple shorter marriages versus one long marriage.

The restricted application strategy that used to let people claim spousal benefits only while letting their own benefit grow was eliminated for people born in 1954 or later, requiring anyone filing for benefits to file for all benefits they're eligible for simultaneously and take the highest one. This deemed filing rule means someone reaching 67 who is eligible for both their own benefit of $1,800 and a spousal benefit of $1,500 automatically gets only the $1,800 because it's higher, and they can't choose to take just the $1,500 spousal benefit while letting their own benefit grow to $2,230 by age 70. The old strategy allowed this kind of gaming to maximize lifetime benefits, but current rules prevent it for most people.

File and suspend used to let people file for benefits to enable their spouse to claim spousal benefits, then immediately suspend their own benefit to earn delayed retirement credits, but this was also eliminated and now suspending benefits also suspends any benefits others are receiving on that record. Someone at full retirement age who wants to delay their own benefit to 70 but allow their spouse to start spousal benefits faces a choice between claiming now so the spouse can get spousal benefits or delaying to 70 but making the spouse wait as well. The elimination of these strategies simplified the system but removed options that some couples used to increase total lifetime benefits.

The do-over provision allows someone who claimed early to repay all benefits received within 12 months of claiming and then re-file later as if the original claim never happened, essentially giving us a one-year window to reverse an early claiming decision if circumstances change. Someone who claimed at 62 and then got a job offer at 62 and 8 months can repay the 8 months of benefits, return to not-claimed status, and re-file later when actually ready to retire. After the 12-month window closes, this option disappears and we're locked into the claiming decision except for the voluntary suspension option that becomes available at full retirement age.

Voluntary suspension at full retirement age lets someone who previously claimed before full retirement age suspend their benefits to earn delayed retirement credits up to age 70, partially reversing an early claiming decision though not fully because the benefit starts from the reduced amount rather than the full PIA. Someone who claimed at 62 getting $1,400 and then suspends at 67 earns 8% annual increases on that $1,400 base, reaching

$1,736 at 70, versus the $2,480 they would have gotten by never claiming until 70. The suspension can make sense for someone who claimed early out of necessity but later no longer needs the income and wants to increase their eventual benefit, though it doesn't undo the early claiming reduction.

Lump sum withdrawal option lets someone at full retirement age who hasn't yet claimed request up to 6 months of retroactive benefits paid as a lump sum, reducing their ongoing monthly benefit to the amount they would have received 6 months earlier. Someone at 67 who files for benefits can request retroactive payment back to 66 and 6 months, receiving a lump sum of 6 months of benefits but permanently locking in the slightly reduced monthly amount from claiming 6 months earlier than full retirement age. This helps people who waited until full retirement age but then faced an unexpected expense and wish they had claimed slightly earlier, giving them a chunk of cash while minimizing the ongoing benefit reduction.

Taxation of benefits based on combined income creates another dimension to claiming strategy because taking Social Security earlier or later affects how much of our other income faces taxation. Someone with $45,000 in IRA withdrawals and $30,000 in Social Security benefits has combined income of $60,000 and 85% of their Social Security gets taxed, while if they delayed Social Security and lived on $60,000 from IRA withdrawals, none of it would be Social Security so the taxation calculation looks completely different. The interaction between Social Security, IRA withdrawals, Roth conversions, and tax brackets creates complex optimization problems that might favor different claiming ages depending on our other resources and tax situation.

The risk of Social Security insolvency and potential benefit cuts affects claiming strategy for people who won't claim for another 10-20 years, because if benefits get cut by 20-25% as projected without Congressional action, the claiming calculus changes. Someone expecting $2,400 per month who plans for only $1,800 because of potential cuts might decide that claiming early looks better since the advantage of delaying shrinks if all benefits get cut proportionally. The counterargument is that even with cuts, delaying still provides the same percentage increase and the longevity insurance value remains, so someone getting 80% of expected benefits at 70 still gets 24% more than they would have gotten at 67 even in the reduced scenario.

The health and family longevity considerations legitimately affect claiming decisions because someone with serious health problems or strong family history of early death faces different probabilities than someone in excellent health from long-lived families. Someone diagnosed with a terminal illness at 63 should probably claim immediately regardless of financial optimization because they won't live long enough for delaying to pay off, while someone in perfect health at 62 with parents who lived to 95 and 98 probably benefits from delaying to maximize the benefit in their likely long retirement. The challenge is that most of us don't know with certainty how long we'll live, and the tendency is to overestimate our knowledge of our own mortality.

The widow's or widower's benefits become available as early as age 60 for people whose spouses died, or age 50 if disabled, and these survivor benefits follow different reduction rules than retirement benefits, making early claiming of survivor benefits less costly than early claiming of retirement benefits in terms of permanent reduction. Someone widowed at 60 can claim survivor benefits at that age receiving 71.5% of what the deceased spouse was receiving or would have received, versus claiming their own retirement benefit at 60 which would incur a 30% reduction. This creates strategies where someone claims survivor benefits at 60 to provide income while letting their own retirement benefit grow to age 70, then switches to their own larger benefit if it exceeds the survivor benefit.

The substantial income needs before full retirement age create legitimate reasons to claim early despite the permanent reduction, and someone who lost their job at 62 with no savings and no other income sources might have no choice but to claim Social Security to avoid homelessness even knowing the reduction hurts them long-term. The optimal claiming strategy assumes we have resources to live on between retirement and claiming, and someone without those resources makes a different calculation where current survival outweighs future optimization. The judgment shouldn't be that they made a mistake by claiming early but that they faced constraints that made early claiming the least bad option.

The spousal and survivor benefit coordination for same-sex married couples works identically to opposite-sex couples following the Supreme Court decision in 2015, meaning same-sex married couples have full access to spousal and survivor benefits based on each other's earnings records as long as they were legally married when one spouse claims or dies. Someone in a same-sex marriage of 15 years has the same spousal benefit rights as someone in an opposite-sex marriage of 15 years, and survivor benefits pass to same-sex surviving spouses just like they would to opposite-sex spouses.

The government pension offset and windfall elimination provision create claiming strategy complications for people affected by them, because someone who worked in non-covered government employment faces reduced or eliminated spousal benefits through GPO and reduced personal benefits through WEP, changing the calculus of when to claim. Someone whose spousal benefit will be eliminated entirely by GPO has no reason to delay their own benefit to preserve spousal benefits since they won't receive spousal benefits anyway, while someone whose benefit will be substantially reduced by WEP might actually benefit more from claiming early since the reduction affects the benefit amount regardless of when they claim.

The overall claiming strategy for most married couples involves the higher earner delaying to 70 to maximize survivor benefits that will support the surviving spouse potentially for decades, while the lower earner can claim anywhere from 62 to full retirement age depending on current income needs since their benefit will likely be replaced by survivor benefits eventually. Single people face a simpler decision based primarily on their own health, longevity expectations, and financial resources, without needing to coordinate with a spouse or optimize for survivor benefits. Someone with poor health and immediate income needs claims early, while someone in good health with adequate resources to delay claims at 70 to maximize lifetime benefits in the likely scenario where they live into their 80s or 90s.

The claiming strategy assumes Social Security stays roughly as promised. Whether that assumption holds depends on what Congress does over the next decade — or doesn't do. The solvency question matters for anyone currently under 55, and planning without some consideration of it is a form of optimism that deserves scrutiny.

What Happens If Congress Does Nothing

The Social Security trust fund is projected to be depleted around 2033-2034 based on current projections from the Social Security trustees, at which point incoming payroll taxes would cover only about 75-80% of scheduled benefits under current law. This doesn't mean Social Security goes away or stops paying anything, just that benefits would need to be cut to match incoming revenue if Congress doesn't act before then, and the system would continue paying reduced benefits indefinitely from ongoing tax collections rather than completely collapsing. Planning for retirement that starts in the 2030s or later requires acknowledging the possibility that benefits might be reduced by 20-25% from current projections, though the political pressure to avoid cuts or find alternative solutions might lead to different outcomes.

The demographic shift driving the funding problem comes from baby boomers retiring in massive numbers while birth rates have declined, creating a situation where there are fewer workers per beneficiary than when the system was designed. In 1960 there were about 5 workers paying taxes for every beneficiary receiving benefits, but by 2024 the ratio dropped to about 2.8 workers per beneficiary, and it's projected to fall to 2.3 by 2040. This means each worker's taxes need to support more beneficiaries than in the past, and either taxes need to increase, benefits need to decrease, or the retirement age needs to rise to reduce the number of beneficiaries relative to workers.

Possible fixes include raising the payroll tax rate from the current 12.4% combined employer-employee rate to perhaps 15% or higher, which would close part of the funding gap but increase costs for workers and employers. Someone earning $60,000 currently pays $3,720 in Social Security tax and their employer pays another $3,720, and raising the rate by 2.6 percentage points would add another $1,560 in annual taxes for both the employee and employer. This addresses the problem but reduces take-home pay for workers and increases employment costs for businesses, creating economic and political resistance that makes the solution difficult despite being mathematically straightforward.

Increasing or eliminating the cap on taxable earnings would subject earnings above the current $168,600 maximum to Social Security taxes, capturing revenue from high earners who currently pay the same absolute amount in taxes as someone earning exactly at the cap. Someone earning $300,000 currently pays $10,453 in Social Security tax just like someone earning $168,600, but eliminating the cap would make them pay $18,600, generating substantial additional revenue from the highest earners. The complication is whether these additional taxes create additional future benefits or not, because the current system links taxes paid to benefits received, and subjecting high earners to unlimited taxes while capping their benefits breaks that linkage and turns Social Security into more of a welfare program.

Raising full retirement age from 67 to 68 or 69 would reduce benefits by making people wait longer to receive unreduced benefits, and it would encourage people to work longer which both increases tax revenue and decreases benefit duration. Someone with full retirement age of 68 instead of 67 who claims at 68 receives the same benefit amount but gets it for one year less, saving the system 12 months of payments, and if they work that extra year they pay an additional year of taxes. The challenge is that raising retirement age disproportionately affects manual laborers and people in physically demanding jobs who might not be able to work until 68 or 69, while office workers and professionals face less burden from the change.

Means-testing benefits for high earners would reduce or eliminate Social Security for people with substantial other income, redirecting those benefits to lower-income retirees or reducing overall system costs. Someone with $200,000 in annual retirement income from pensions, investments, and other sources might see their Social Security reduced or phased out entirely, while someone with only Social Security and modest savings would receive full benefits. This transforms Social Security from social insurance where everyone pays in and everyone receives benefits to a welfare program where benefits depend on need, breaking the political coalition that has protected the program by ensuring that even wealthy people have a stake in maintaining benefits.

Changing the inflation adjustment formula from the current CPI-W to something that grows more slowly, like chained CPI, would reduce the annual cost of living adjustments and cause benefits to fall behind inflation gradually over time. Someone receiving $2,000 per month today might receive $2,060 next year under current COLA but only $2,050 under chained CPI, a difference that seems small initially but compounds over 20-30 years into benefits that are several percentage points lower than under current law. This stealth benefit cut affects current retirees as well as future ones, and it particularly harms the oldest beneficiaries who have received decades of slightly lower COLAs.

Each approach creates different winners and losers and faces political resistance from affected groups, and the longer Congress waits to act, the more severe the eventual changes will need to be. Raising the retirement age by one year is politically difficult now but might need to be two years if Congress waits another decade to address the problem, and raising the payroll tax by 2 percentage points is hard to sell but becomes 3 percentage points if delayed. The political incentive is to kick the problem down the road and let future Congresses deal with it, which has worked so far but can't continue indefinitely as the trust fund depletion date approaches.

Planning for reduced benefits means doing retirement calculations with Social Security at 75% of currently projected amounts, which requires more personal savings to make up the difference between what we expect and what we might actually receive. Someone expecting $2,400 per month who plans for only $1,800 needs an extra $600 per month from savings, or $7,200 per year, which at 4% withdrawal rate requires $180,000 more in portfolio. For a couple expecting $3,600 combined, planning for $2,700 requires $270,000 extra saved, and for someone who is 35 now planning retirement in 30 years, this extra savings needs to start immediately to have enough time to accumulate the additional amount.

The conservative approach assumes benefits will be cut and plans accordingly, accepting that we might end up with more money than strictly needed if Congress fixes the problem and benefits don't get reduced, while the optimistic approach assumes Congress will fix the problem and plans for full scheduled benefits, risking shortfall if cuts actually happen. Someone who saves an extra $180,000 assuming benefit cuts and then receives full benefits has extra money they can spend on luxuries, help family, or leave to heirs, while someone who assumes full benefits and receives cuts faces potential hardship in their 80s when they're least able to work or recover from financial problems.

The political reality is that Social Security cuts affect tens of millions of voters who reliably turn out in elections, creating enormous pressure on Congress to avoid cuts or find alternative solutions that don't reduce benefits for current or near-retirees. Someone who is 55 or older might reasonably expect that Congress will protect their benefits even if younger workers face changes, because politicians fear the electoral consequences of cutting benefits for people already in or near retirement. Someone who is 35 faces higher likelihood that their benefits will be modified since they don't start receiving benefits for another 30 years and politicians can more easily justify changes that only affect future beneficiaries.

The taxation of benefits could change as part of a solution package, potentially raising revenue by making more benefits taxable or adjusting the income thresholds that haven't been updated since 1984. The thresholds of $25,000 for singles and $32,000 for couples meant something different in 1984 than they do in 2024, and adjusting them for inflation would be around $73,000 and $93,000 respectively, meaning far fewer people would face benefit taxation if the thresholds had been indexed. Congress could raise revenue by leaving the thresholds where they are so that over time more benefits become taxable as incomes rise, or they could make benefits more heavily taxable for high earners as part of de facto means-testing.

Immigration policy affects Social Security solvency because additional workers paying taxes improve the worker-to-beneficiary ratio, and higher immigration creates more tax revenue without immediately increasing benefit obligations since immigrants need to work for years to qualify for benefits. Someone who immigrates at age 30 and works for 40 years paying Social Security taxes only starts receiving benefits at 70, paying in much more than they'll likely receive over their shorter benefit period, while someone born in the U.S. might receive benefits for 30+ years after working similar lengths. The political toxicity of immigration makes this solution difficult to implement even though it's mathematically one of the more straightforward ways to improve system finances.

Benefit taxation revenue currently goes back into the Social Security trust fund, providing one of the sources of income beyond payroll taxes, and changes to how benefits are taxed or what happens to that revenue could affect solvency projections. Someone paying $3,000 in taxes on their Social Security benefits contributes that $3,000 to the trust fund, helping to extend its life, and if Congress eliminated benefit taxation as part of a tax reform package, it would worsen the funding gap unless replaced with alternative revenue. The complexity of the taxation formula and its increasing reach as incomes rise creates a stealth tax increase that helps fund the system without requiring explicit payroll tax rate increases.

Private account proposals that would let workers direct some of their payroll taxes into personal accounts have been debated but never implemented, facing concerns about transition costs, market risk, and the fundamental change from social insurance to personal responsibility. Someone who invested their Social Security taxes in stocks in 2000 and retired in 2009 would have faced terrible timing and possibly inadequate retirement income, while someone who invested in 1990 and retired in 2010 would have benefited from strong returns. The guaranteed nature of traditional Social Security benefits provides protection against market timing that private accounts don't offer, though supporters argue the higher expected returns from stock investments outweigh the additional risk.

The interaction with Medicare creates additional pressure because Medicare faces its own funding challenges on a similar timeline, and Congress likely needs to address both programs simultaneously rather than fixing Social Security in isolation. Someone who reaches 65 in 2035 faces potentially reduced Social Security benefits and potentially modified Medicare coverage with higher costs, and the combination of both programs being in crisis creates greater urgency but also makes the political solution more complex because any changes affect more people in more ways.

State and local government pensions facing funding problems create pressure on Social Security because governments might reduce pension benefits or require workers to rely more heavily on Social Security, increasing the strain on the federal system. Someone with a state pension that gets cut from $30,000 to $20,000 needs an extra $10,000 annually from Social Security to maintain their lifestyle, and if millions of state and local workers face similar cuts, the pressure on Social Security to make up the difference increases even as its own funding remains shaky.

We can't control whether Congress fixes Social Security or how they choose to fix it, but we can control our personal savings rate and retirement spending expectations to be resilient to whatever actually happens. Someone who builds retirement plans assuming full scheduled benefits and makes no alternative preparations faces potential hardship if benefits get cut, while someone who saves extra and plans for reduced benefits has a cushion that makes them more resilient to whatever Congress decides. The worst case is that benefits don't get cut and we have more money than we strictly needed, which creates options for helping family, donating to causes we care about, or spending more on travel and experiences, all of which beat running out of money because we counted on benefits that got reduced.

The information available to plan for Social Security changes is limited to speculation and proposals rather than concrete legislation, making it hard to know exactly what to prepare for. Someone who is 45 and planning retirement in 20 years can see various proposals that include raising retirement age, means-testing benefits, increasing taxes, and cutting benefits, but they don't know which if any will actually pass. The reasonable approach is to plan for partial benefit cuts of perhaps 20% and consider any benefits above that level a bonus rather than counting on full scheduled benefits and hoping Congress fixes everything.

The risk-reward calculation for different planning assumptions suggests that conservative assumptions with extra savings hurt less if wrong than optimistic assumptions with minimal savings. Someone who saves an extra $200,000 assuming benefit cuts who then receives full benefits has money to spend or give away, experiencing the relatively pleasant problem of having more than needed. Someone who saves nothing extra assuming full benefits who then faces 25% cuts has genuine financial hardship in their 80s with no good options to fix it, experiencing the catastrophic problem of poverty in old age. The asymmetry of these outcomes argues strongly for conservative planning even if it means working a few more years or saving more aggressively than might strictly be necessary.

The generation most affected by potential changes is people currently in their 30s and 40s who won't reach retirement age until the 2040s or later, well after the trust fund depletion date and into the period where modifications are most likely to be implemented. Someone who is 35 in 2024 reaches age 67 in 2056, two decades after the projected trust fund exhaustion, and they should assume their benefits will look different from current law projections. Someone who is 60 in 2024 reaches 67 in 2031, before trust fund depletion, and might reasonably expect that political pressure will preserve their benefits even if younger workers face changes.

The trust fund accounting mechanics matter less than the political will to maintain benefits, because the government could simply appropriate general revenue to make up shortfalls if Congress decides that's preferable to cutting benefits. Someone entitled to $2,400 per month cares about receiving $2,400 per month regardless of whether it comes from payroll taxes, trust fund drawdown, or general revenue appropriations, and the source of the funding is a technical accounting issue rather than a limitation on what Congress could do if they chose. The question is whether political pressure to avoid benefit cuts overcomes pressure to avoid tax increases or deficit spending, and that's ultimately a political question rather than a mathematical one.

Social Security is one income source. Healthcare is one of the largest expenses. And for anyone planning to retire before 65, the gap between leaving employer coverage and reaching Medicare is one of the most financially dangerous periods in the entire retirement timeline. The ACA was designed to fill that gap — but it rewards people who understand how it works and punishes people who don't.

The Healthcare Gap

The Affordable Care Act marketplace provides health insurance for people who don't have employer coverage or Medicare, and it becomes critically important for anyone planning to retire before 65 when Medicare eligibility begins, because we need health insurance for the gap years between leaving employer coverage and qualifying for Medicare. Someone retiring at 60 faces five years of needing to purchase individual health insurance, and the costs and subsidy structures under the ACA create both opportunities and traps that can make or break an early retirement plan depending on how well we understand and navigate the system.

Premiums in the individual market vary dramatically by age, location, and income, with a 60-year-old paying roughly three times what a 30-year-old pays for the same coverage in the same location, and geographic differences creating situations where identical coverage costs $800 per month in one state and $1,500 per month in another. Someone who is 60 living in a low-cost area might pay $700 per month for silver-level coverage before subsidies, while someone the same age in a high-cost metro area pays $1,400 per month, and these differences persist even after accounting for cost of living because health insurance pricing doesn't perfectly track housing costs or general price levels.

The subsidy structure ties premium assistance to income using Modified Adjusted Gross Income as the reference point, and the subsidies phase in and out based on Federal Poverty Level thresholds that change annually but currently sit around $15,060 for singles and $20,440 for couples. Someone with MAGI below 150% of FPL pays very little for silver coverage through enhanced subsidies, while someone with MAGI between 150% and 400% of FPL receives sliding-scale subsidies that reduce premiums to 2-8.5% of income, and someone above 400% of FPL receives no subsidies and pays full price for coverage which might be $15,000-25,000 annually for a couple in their early 60s.

MAGI for ACA purposes includes wages, self-employment income, taxable interest and dividends, pension and annuity income, rental income, taxable Social Security benefits, and Traditional IRA or 401k withdrawals, but it excludes Roth IRA withdrawals, HSA withdrawals for medical expenses, return of basis from non-qualified annuities, municipal bond interest, and several other income types. This creates enormous opportunities for people with the right asset mix to manipulate their MAGI to qualify for subsidies by living on Roth withdrawals and taxable account principal while keeping Traditional IRA withdrawals low enough to stay under subsidy thresholds.

Someone with $800,000 split evenly between Traditional IRA and Roth IRA who needs $50,000 to live on can take $10,000 from Traditional IRA showing that as MAGI and take $40,000 from Roth showing zero MAGI, creating reported income of only $10,000 that qualifies for maximum subsidies. The same person taking $50,000 from Traditional IRA shows $50,000 MAGI and might get reduced subsidies or no subsidies depending on their age and location, potentially paying $10,000-15,000 more annually in premiums for making the wrong withdrawal choice. This makes Roth accounts incredibly valuable for early retirees not just for the tax-free growth but for the MAGI flexibility that affects ACA subsidies.

The subsidy cliff that existed before 2021 would have cut off subsidies completely at 400% of FPL, creating situations where earning one extra dollar could cost thousands in lost subsidies, but the American Rescue Plan and Inflation Reduction Act extended and enhanced subsidies through at least 2025 with no upper income limit, capping premiums at 8.5% of income even for high earners. Someone earning $60,000 who would have paid $18,000 in premiums without the expansion now pays a maximum of $5,100, saving $12,900 annually through the enhanced subsidies, and whether these enhancements continue past 2025 depends on Congressional action that's uncertain as of this writing.

If the subsidy enhancements expire and the 400% FPL cliff returns, someone with MAGI of $62,000 single or $84,000 married in 2025 would lose all subsidies and face full-price premiums that might be $12,000-20,000 annually, while someone with MAGI of $61,000 or $83,000 would receive substantial subsidies and pay only $4,000-6,000. This creates enormous incentive to manage MAGI carefully to stay under the threshold if it returns, potentially through strategic Roth conversions in high-income working years, moving to lower-cost locations to reduce needed MAGI, or structuring withdrawals to minimize taxable income.

The metal tiers of bronze, silver, gold, and platinum determine cost-sharing through deductibles and copays, with bronze plans having the lowest premiums but highest out-of-pocket costs and platinum having the highest premiums but lowest out-of-pocket costs. A silver plan for a 60-year-old might cost $700 per month with a $3,000 deductible and $8,000 out-of-pocket maximum, while a bronze plan costs $550 per month with a $7,000 deductible and $9,000 maximum, and the choice depends on expected healthcare utilization and risk tolerance for high potential costs.

Someone in excellent health who rarely uses healthcare might save $1,800 annually by choosing bronze over silver, and if they have no healthcare expenses that year, they come out ahead by the premium savings. Someone with chronic conditions requiring expensive medications and regular specialist visits will hit their deductible and out-of-pocket maximum regardless of plan choice, and paying higher premiums for gold or platinum coverage that reduces copays and coinsurance might save money overall. The calculation requires estimating annual healthcare costs including prescriptions, doctor visits, and procedures, then comparing total annual cost including both premiums and out-of-pocket expenses across different metal tiers.

The silver plan's importance comes from Cost Sharing Reductions that are only available on silver plans for people with MAGI below 250% of FPL, creating situations where a subsidized silver plan costs less in total annual expense than a bronze plan despite higher sticker premiums. Someone with MAGI at 200% of FPL gets a silver plan with reduced cost-sharing that might have a $500 deductible and $2,000 out-of-pocket maximum instead of the standard $3,000 and $8,000, and combined with premium subsidies, this enhanced silver plan might cost $1,200 in annual premiums plus typical out-of-pocket costs versus $2,400 for bronze with higher cost-sharing.

The narrow networks that many ACA plans use to control costs mean we might not have access to the doctors and hospitals we prefer, and someone accustomed to employer PPO coverage with broad networks might be shocked by ACA HMO networks that exclude major medical centers or require referrals for specialists. Checking whether our current doctors participate in a plan's network before enrolling matters more than the metal tier or premium cost, because saving $200 per month on premiums is meaningless if we then have to drive 50 miles to find an in-network primary care doctor or can't see the specialist managing our chronic condition.

Out-of-pocket maximums provide a cap on annual healthcare costs excluding premiums, protecting against catastrophic medical bills that could otherwise bankrupt us, and someone with a $9,000 out-of-pocket maximum knows their worst-case total annual healthcare cost is premiums plus $9,000. The comfort of knowing that a serious illness or injury can't cost more than $9,000 plus premiums makes higher-deductible plans with lower premiums more palatable for people with adequate emergency savings to cover the out-of-pocket maximum if needed, while someone without $9,000 in accessible savings might need a plan with lower deductibles and out-of-pocket costs even if it means higher premiums.

Prescription drug coverage varies substantially between plans even within the same metal tier, and someone taking expensive medications needs to check whether their specific drugs are covered on the plan formulary and what tier they're placed in, because the difference between generic copays of $10 and specialty tier coinsurance of 30% creates enormous cost differences. Someone taking a brand-name drug that costs $800 per month might pay $25 copay on one plan's formulary and $240 coinsurance on another plan, creating $2,580 annual difference that swamps any premium savings from choosing the cheaper plan.

The Special Enrollment Period rules determine when we can sign up for coverage outside the annual open enrollment window that runs November through January, and qualifying events include losing employer coverage, moving to a new state, marriage, divorce, and birth or adoption of a child. Someone who retires in July can enroll in ACA coverage immediately upon losing employer coverage without waiting for open enrollment, but someone who simply quits working without losing coverage or who maintains COBRA after leaving employment might not qualify for special enrollment and could face months without coverage until the next open enrollment period.

COBRA continuation coverage from a previous employer lets us keep employer plan coverage for 18 months after leaving the job by paying the full premium plus 2% administrative fee, and this creates both a bridge option and a comparison point for ACA coverage. Someone whose employer plan costs $800 per month fully loaded might face $2,000 per month COBRA premium because they're now paying both the employer and employee portions, and at 60 years old they might find ACA coverage with subsidies costs $500-700 per month for comparable coverage, making COBRA obviously worse. Someone at 50 with low MAGI might find COBRA costs $1,200 per month versus $300 for subsidized ACA coverage, again making ACA the clear choice.

The marriage penalty in ACA subsidies creates situations where two people living together receive larger combined subsidies if unmarried than if married, because each person filing separately claims their own income against single FPL thresholds rather than combining into married thresholds that aren't quite double the single amounts. Two people each with MAGI of $35,000 filing as singles might each receive substantial subsidies, while married filing jointly with combined MAGI of $70,000 they receive smaller subsidies because married FPL thresholds are only about 35% higher than single thresholds despite double the people and income. This creates perverse incentives for couples to delay marriage or even divorce for subsidy purposes, though the benefits need to be substantial to justify the legal and personal complications.

The income verification process requires us to estimate our MAGI for the upcoming year when we apply for coverage, and if our actual income differs from our estimate, we reconcile the difference when filing taxes, either receiving additional subsidy as a tax credit or repaying excess subsidies. Someone who estimated $40,000 MAGI and received subsidies based on that amount but actually earned $55,000 has to repay some or all of the excess subsidies when filing taxes, potentially creating a tax bill of thousands of dollars. Conversely, someone who estimated $55,000 but only earned $40,000 receives additional subsidy as a refundable tax credit, getting money back at tax time.

The repayment caps limit how much excess subsidy we have to repay if we underestimated income, ranging from $325 for someone under 200% of FPL to $2,800 for someone over 400% of FPL, and these caps provide some protection against catastrophic tax bills from income fluctuations. Someone who estimated $45,000 income and received $8,000 in subsidies but actually earned $75,000 might have received $3,000 too much in subsidies based on actual income, but they only have to repay $2,800 because of the cap, leaving them $200 ahead despite the substantial underestimate. These repayment caps don't exist if the subsidy enhancements expire and we end up above 400% of FPL, making accurate income estimation more important if cliff returns.

The estimated income that determines monthly subsidies should be conservative for people with variable income to avoid surprise repayment at tax time, and someone with uncertain retirement income from consulting or part-time work might estimate on the high side knowing they can claim additional subsidy at tax time if actual income is lower. The pain of repaying $2,000 at tax time because we underestimated income outweighs the benefit of receiving $2,000 in extra monthly subsidy that we then have to return, because most people prefer lower monthly premiums to tax-time windfalls, but the asymmetric caps make underestimating slightly less painful than overestimating.

Geographic arbitrage becomes even more valuable when considering ACA premiums because moving from a high-cost state to a low-cost state might save $500-800 per month in healthcare premiums for a couple in their early 60s, adding to housing and tax savings from the move. Someone paying $2,000 per month for ACA coverage in California or New York might pay $1,200 per month for comparable coverage in Florida or Texas, saving $9,600 annually on healthcare alone before accounting for lower housing costs and potentially lower state taxes. The healthcare savings from geographic moves can exceed the housing savings for people in expensive insurance markets, making location choice critical for early retirement feasibility.

The strategy for early retirees involves building Roth balances during working years so we can live on Roth withdrawals while keeping MAGI low for ACA subsidies, possibly doing Roth conversions in high-income working years even if it increases current taxes because it creates tax-free income sources later. Someone who converts $100,000 from Traditional to Roth over several years pays perhaps $24,000 in extra taxes during those conversions but creates $100,000 that can be withdrawn tax-free in early retirement, keeping MAGI low enough to qualify for $10,000-15,000 annually in ACA subsidies from 60-65. The subsidy benefit over five years totals $50,000-75,000, substantially exceeding the $24,000 cost of the conversions.

The interaction between MAGI management for ACA subsidies and tax planning for Roth conversions creates complex optimization problems where we want low MAGI during ACA years but might want to do conversions in the years immediately before or after to move money to Roth without giving up subsidies. Someone retiring at 58 might do aggressive Roth conversions from 58-60 before ACA subsidies start mattering, showing MAGI of $80,000-100,000 and paying taxes on those conversions, then dramatically reduce MAGI to $30,000-40,000 from 60-65 by living on the converted Roth money plus taxable account withdrawals. After 65 when Medicare begins, they can resume Roth conversions if desired without affecting ACA subsidies that no longer matter.

The risk of subsidy changes or elimination makes depending entirely on subsidies for affordable healthcare dangerous for early retirement planning, and someone whose retirement plan only works if they receive $12,000 annually in subsidies faces catastrophic failure if Congress eliminates or substantially reduces those subsidies. Building retirement plans with some cushion that work even with reduced subsidies or at full-price premiums provides resilience against policy changes, though someone with adequate cushion might rationally claim subsidies when available while having backup plans if they disappear.

The asset test nonexistence in ACA subsidies means someone with $2 million in retirement accounts still qualifies for subsidies if their MAGI is low enough, creating situations where wealthy people receive government assistance for healthcare while their net worth exceeds most Americans. This differs from means-tested programs like Medicaid that look at both income and assets, and the policy choice to base subsidies only on MAGI reflects both administrative simplicity and the reality that assets aren't spendable income until converted to withdrawals that then show up as MAGI.

The permanent expansion of subsidies or return of the cliff depends on Congressional action that we can't predict, making planning for both scenarios prudent by having strategies that work under either scenario rather than betting everything on one outcome. Someone who needs subsidies to afford early retirement should have contingency plans for what they'll do if subsidies disappear, whether that's working longer, moving to a cheaper area, accepting higher healthcare costs by reducing other spending, or finding part-time employment with health benefits to bridge the gap to 65.

At 65, Medicare begins. It seems simpler than the ACA marketplace. It isn't, particularly for anyone trying to minimize lifetime healthcare costs while preserving access to good care. The basics of how Medicare is structured shape everything that comes after.

How Medicare Works

Medicare eligibility begins at age 65 for most people regardless of retirement status, and we can enroll during a seven-month window starting three months before the month we turn 65, but missing this window triggers late enrollment penalties that last forever and increase our premiums permanently. Someone who turns 65 in June can enroll anytime from March through September without penalty, while someone who misses this window and enrolls a year late faces a 10% penalty on Part B premiums for the rest of their life, adding roughly $18 per month or $216 annually to their Medicare costs in perpetuity.

Part A covers hospital stays, skilled nursing facility care, hospice, and some home health services, and it's premium-free for people who worked at least 10 years paying Medicare taxes or whose spouse did, making it essentially free for most Americans who paid into the system during their working years. Someone hospitalized for surgery uses Part A to cover the hospital costs after a deductible of $1,632 in 2024, and if the stay extends beyond 60 days, daily copays kick in starting at $408 per day for days 61-90 and $816 per day for lifetime reserve days beyond 90, creating substantial out-of-pocket costs for extended hospitalizations.

Part B covers doctor visits, outpatient care, preventive services, medical equipment, and some medications administered in medical settings, and it requires a monthly premium of $174.70 in 2024 for most people though high earners pay more through Income-Related Monthly Adjustment Amounts that can push premiums to $594 per month. Someone with Modified Adjusted Gross Income above $103,000 single or $206,000 married faces IRMAA surcharges that add $70-419 per month to their Part B premium, and these surcharges look back two years at tax returns, so someone retiring at 65 in 2024 pays IRMAA based on their 2022 income when they were likely still working full-time at high salary.

The two-year lookback for IRMAA creates problems for new retirees who earned substantial income two years ago but now have much lower income, and while appeals exist for life-changing events like retirement, the default is paying surcharges based on old high income rather than current low income. Someone who earned $150,000 in 2022 and retired in 2023 with $40,000 retirement income pays IRMAA in 2024 based on the $150,000 despite their income dropping by more than half, adding $769 annually to Medicare costs that wouldn't apply if the lookback period was shorter or if the life-changing event appeal was automatic.

Part B premiums get deducted from Social Security benefits for people who are receiving Social Security when they enroll in Part B, automatically reducing the monthly Social Security check by the premium amount and simplifying payment by avoiding separate billing. Someone receiving $2,000 per month in Social Security with standard Part B premium of $174.70 nets $1,825.30 after the premium deduction, and if they face IRMAA surcharges, those also get deducted automatically, potentially reducing the net Social Security to $1,400-1,600 depending on the surcharge amount.

Part C or Medicare Advantage provides an alternative to Original Medicare where private insurance companies offer plans that combine Part A, Part B, and usually Part D prescription drug coverage plus sometimes dental and vision, often with $0 additional premium beyond the Part B premium we're already paying. These plans restrict us to network providers like HMOs and require referrals and prior authorizations that Original Medicare doesn't, but they cap out-of-pocket expenses at maximums like $5,000-8,000 annually versus the unlimited potential costs under Original Medicare, creating trade-offs between flexibility and cost protection.

Someone choosing Medicare Advantage gets all their care through the plan's network and follows the plan's rules for referrals and approvals, paying copays for doctor visits and procedures that are often lower than the 20% coinsurance under Original Medicare, but they can't go outside the network except for emergencies without paying full costs themselves. A retired couple might pay $0 additional premium for a Medicare Advantage plan beyond their Part B premiums and face $6,500 out-of-pocket maximum each, knowing their worst-case annual cost is $174.70 times 24 months plus $13,000, or about $17,200 for the couple.

Part D covers prescription drugs through private plans that require separate enrollment and premium payment, and the coverage includes a deductible phase, initial coverage phase, coverage gap or donut hole, and catastrophic phase with different copays and coinsurance at each stage. Someone taking expensive medications might pay $545 annual deductible, then 25% coinsurance until reaching $5,030 in total drug costs, then higher coinsurance in the coverage gap until hitting catastrophic threshold of $8,000 in out-of-pocket costs, at which point they pay minimal copays or coinsurance for the rest of the year.

The formularies that Part D plans use to determine which drugs are covered and at what tier create enormous variation in annual drug costs between plans even when the premiums are similar, and someone taking three maintenance medications needs to check each plan's formulary to see if their specific drugs are covered and what tier they're in. A plan with $35 monthly premium might place all three drugs in low tiers with $15 copays each, creating $45 monthly drug cost plus $35 premium for $80 total, while a plan with $25 monthly premium might place the same drugs in higher tiers with $80 total copay, creating $105 monthly cost despite the lower premium.

Medigap or Medicare Supplement plans work with Original Medicare to fill the gaps in coverage, paying the deductibles, copays, and coinsurance that Parts A and B don't cover, and they're sold by private insurers at premiums that vary by plan type, age, location, and company. Plan G is the most comprehensive and popular option for new enrollees, covering everything except the Part B deductible of $240 annually, and premiums range from $150-250 per month depending on age and location, creating total monthly Medicare costs of roughly $325-425 including the Part B premium.

Someone with Plan G pays the $240 Part B deductible each year and then has essentially zero out-of-pocket costs for Medicare-covered services for the rest of the year, because the Medigap plan covers the 20% coinsurance and any other cost-sharing. A person using $50,000 in Medicare services during a year pays the $240 deductible plus $2,095 in Part B premiums plus perhaps $2,400 in Plan G premiums for total cost of $4,735, versus potentially $10,000 or more in coinsurance without the Medigap plan if they had to pay 20% of all services out of pocket.

The choice between Medicare Advantage and Original Medicare with Medigap depends on risk tolerance, desire for provider flexibility, and willingness to pay higher premiums for lower out-of-pocket costs, and someone who wants to choose any doctor without referrals and doesn't want to worry about coinsurance pays more in monthly premiums for Original Medicare plus Medigap but has nearly unlimited provider access and minimal out-of-pocket costs. Someone who is comfortable with networks and referrals in exchange for lower premiums and capped out-of-pocket expenses chooses Medicare Advantage, potentially saving $2,000-3,000 annually in premiums but facing more restrictions on care.

The guaranteed issue rights for Medigap only exist during the six-month window starting when we first enroll in Part B at 65 or older, and after that window closes, insurance companies can deny coverage or charge higher premiums based on health status, making the initial enrollment decision critical. Someone who chooses Medicare Advantage at 65 and then wants to switch to Medigap at 70 after developing health problems might be denied coverage or face premiums of $400-500 per month instead of the $200 they would have paid at 65, effectively locking them into Medicare Advantage once they miss the guaranteed issue window.

The Medigap Plan N offers a lower-cost alternative to Plan G by requiring copays of up to $20 for office visits and $50 for emergency room visits that don't result in admission, and premiums run about $20-40 less per month than Plan G, making it attractive for people who don't visit doctors frequently. Someone with Plan N might pay $180 monthly premium instead of $220 for Plan G, saving $480 annually in premiums, and if they have 10 doctor visits during the year at $20 each, they pay $200 in copays for net savings of $280 compared to Plan G.

Part A enrollment becomes automatic for people who are already receiving Social Security when they turn 65, and they get enrolled without taking any action, while people who haven't yet claimed Social Security need to actively enroll in Part A and Part B during their initial enrollment period. Someone who claimed Social Security at 62 gets automatically enrolled in Medicare at 65 and receives their Medicare card a few months before their 65th birthday, while someone working until 68 who hasn't claimed Social Security needs to sign up for Medicare separately through the Social Security website or office.

The working past 65 with employer coverage creates special rules where we can delay Part B enrollment without penalty as long as we maintain creditable employer coverage through a company with 20 or more employees, and we then get a special enrollment period when we leave the job or lose the employer coverage. Someone working until 68 with employer health insurance doesn't need to enroll in Part B at 65 and can delay until they actually retire at 68, saving three years of Part B premiums totaling about $6,300, but if their employer has fewer than 20 employees, the employer coverage isn't creditable and they should enroll in Part B at 65 to avoid penalties.

The creditable coverage determination matters because maintaining creditable prescription drug coverage from an employer or union allows us to delay Part D enrollment without penalty, while going without creditable drug coverage for 63 days or longer triggers a late enrollment penalty of 1% of the national base premium for each month we were without coverage. Someone who retires at 65, loses employer drug coverage, but doesn't enroll in Part D for two years faces 24% permanent penalty on Part D premiums, adding roughly $8 per month to Part D costs forever, and this penalty continues for as long as they have Part D coverage.

The Medicare and employer coverage coordination depends on employer size, with Medicare becoming primary payer and employer coverage secondary for retirees or employees at small companies, while employer coverage remains primary and Medicare becomes secondary for active employees at large companies with 20 or more employees. Someone working at a large company at 65 can choose to delay Part B enrollment and rely entirely on employer coverage, or they can enroll in both and have the employer plan supplement Medicare, but the latter approach means paying both Part B premiums and any employee contribution to employer coverage without necessarily getting better total coverage.

HSA contribution eligibility ends when we enroll in any part of Medicare, and this creates planning considerations around when to sign up for Medicare versus continuing to work and contribute to HSA. Someone who turns 65 while still working and wants to keep contributing to their HSA should delay Medicare enrollment as long as they have creditable employer coverage, because signing up for Part A even while not using it makes them ineligible for HSA contributions. The confusion around Medicare and HSA rules has led some people to unknowingly violate the prohibition by contributing to HSA after Medicare enrollment, creating excess contributions requiring correction.

The automatic Part A enrollment when claiming Social Security affects HSA contributions because someone who claims Social Security at 64 gets automatically enrolled in Part A at 65, and the enrollment is retroactive for six months, meaning they may have made ineligible HSA contributions during those six months without realizing it. Someone who plans to work past 65 and continue HSA contributions should delay claiming Social Security until they're ready to stop HSA contributions, or they need to decline Part A during the Social Security application process which requires specific action and awareness of the interaction.

The Medicare Savings Programs for low-income beneficiaries can pay Medicare premiums and sometimes cost-sharing for people with income below roughly 135% of federal poverty level and limited assets, effectively making Medicare free or very low-cost for qualifying individuals. Someone with income of $18,000 annually and assets under $9,430 might qualify for programs that pay their Part B premium and Part D premium plus eliminate cost-sharing, creating essentially free comprehensive healthcare coverage, but the asset limits exclude many middle-class retirees who have retirement savings above the thresholds even with modest income.

The Extra Help program for Part D reduces or eliminates prescription drug costs for people with limited income and resources, paying the Part D premium, eliminating the deductible, and reducing copays to $4-10 per prescription for people who qualify. Someone with income under $23,000 single or $31,000 married and assets under $16,000 or $32,000 gets automatic Extra Help that dramatically reduces drug costs, potentially saving thousands annually for people taking multiple expensive medications, but again the asset limits exclude most people with retirement accounts.

Medicare costs for a healthy couple both age 65 might be $350 per month each for Part B premiums plus $200 each for Medigap Plan G plus $35 each for Part D for total of $1,170 monthly or $14,040 annually, and this assumes no IRMAA surcharges and no significant out-of-pocket costs beyond the Part B deductible. Someone choosing Medicare Advantage instead might pay only $350 per month each for Part B with the rest included in the $0 premium Advantage plan for total of $700 monthly or $8,400 annually, saving $5,640 in exchange for network restrictions and potential out-of-pocket costs up to the plan maximum.

The annual enrollment period from October 15 to December 7 allows changes to Medicare Advantage and Part D plans with changes effective January 1, and reviewing plans annually makes sense because formularies change, premiums change, and our health status and medication needs change. Someone who chose a plan in 2020 based on medications they were taking then might find in 2024 that their current medications are no longer covered or have moved to higher tiers, making a different plan more cost-effective, and the annual review ensures we're in the most appropriate plan for current circumstances.

The trial right for Medicare Advantage allows someone to try a Medicare Advantage plan for up to 12 months and then switch to Original Medicare with guaranteed Medigap coverage if they decide Advantage isn't working for them, but this only works during the first year of Medicare Advantage enrollment. Someone who starts Medicare Advantage at 65 can switch to Original Medicare plus Medigap anytime in the first 12 months without medical underwriting, but after that first year they lose the guaranteed right to Medigap coverage and face potential denials or high premiums based on health status.

Understanding what Medicare covers tells us what it costs at the base level. Planning for what it costs over 20 or 30 years of retirement — including the income-based surcharges that many retirees trigger without realizing it — is a different and more expensive conversation.

The Real Cost of Getting Older

IRMAA surcharges add dramatically to Medicare costs for people with higher income, using Modified Adjusted Gross Income from two years prior to determine whether we pay the standard Part B premium of $174.70 per month or surcharges ranging from $244.60 to $594 monthly, and Part D also faces IRMAA surcharges ranging from $12.90 to $81 monthly on top of the plan premium. Someone with MAGI above $103,000 single or $206,000 married in 2022 pays IRMAA in 2024, and the surcharges increase in steps at higher income levels, with the top tier starting at $500,000 single or $750,000 married where combined Part B and Part D surcharges reach $675 per month or $8,100 annually per person.

The two-year lookback creates planning opportunities and problems because our income two years before Medicare enrollment might not reflect our current retirement income, and someone retiring at 65 who earned $150,000 at age 63 pays IRMAA at 65 based on that high working income even though their retirement income is only $50,000. The appeals process allows us to request IRMAA reduction based on life-changing events including retirement, work reduction, loss of pension, divorce, or death of spouse, and filing Form SSA-44 with documentation of the event can reduce or eliminate IRMAA surcharges based on current income rather than the two-year-old tax return.

Someone who retired in 2023 with their last full year of work showing $140,000 MAGI can appeal their 2024 IRMAA by providing documentation that they're no longer working and their current income is much lower, potentially saving $2,000-4,000 annually in surcharges they shouldn't be paying given actual current circumstances. The appeal requires proactive action and documentation rather than happening automatically, and many new retirees pay unnecessary IRMAA for a year or more before discovering they could have appealed, wasting thousands in excess Medicare premiums.

Roth conversions in the two years before Medicare enrollment can trigger IRMAA surcharges that make the conversions much more expensive than anticipated, and someone doing aggressive Roth conversions at 63 showing $120,000 MAGI from conversions faces IRMAA at 65 that adds $1,500-2,500 to annual Medicare costs, reducing the benefit of the conversion. The strategy of doing conversions either before age 63 or after age 67 when the converted amounts won't trigger IRMAA during initial Medicare enrollment makes sense for people planning conversions, though once we're past the initial enrollment period, IRMAA from conversions might be worth accepting if the long-term tax benefits outweigh two years of higher Medicare premiums.

The income brackets for IRMAA adjust annually for inflation, and the thresholds in 2024 of $103,000 single or $206,000 married for the first surcharge tier will be slightly higher in 2025 and beyond, creating moving targets for income planning. Someone managing income to stay just under the IRMAA threshold needs to track the annual adjustments and keep their MAGI under the updated amounts, and income that's $5,000 under the threshold in one year might trigger IRMAA the next year if the threshold doesn't increase as much as the income source.

Strategic Roth conversions during the first few years of retirement before RMDs begin can reduce lifetime Medicare costs by moving money from Traditional to Roth accounts that don't create MAGI when withdrawn later, and someone who converts $200,000 from Traditional IRA to Roth from ages 65-70 pays IRMAA during those conversion years but then has $200,000 in Roth that can be withdrawn from 73 onward without triggering IRMAA. The RMDs that would have come from that $200,000 Traditional IRA might have pushed them into IRMAA brackets from 73-85, costing $2,000-3,000 annually in surcharges for potentially 12 years or $24,000-36,000 total, which might exceed the IRMAA costs during the conversion years.

The calculation of whether to accept IRMAA during conversions versus accepting IRMAA from RMDs later depends on how long we expect to live, what tax brackets we face during conversion years versus RMD years, and whether the conversions move us into higher IRMAA tiers or just extend time in lower tiers. Someone whose RMDs will keep them in the first IRMAA tier from 73-90 pays roughly $2,000 annually in surcharges for 17 years totaling $34,000, while converting enough to eliminate those RMDs might create $3,000 annually in IRMAA for 5 conversion years totaling $15,000, saving $19,000 in lifetime Medicare costs in addition to any income tax savings from the conversions.

Medicare Advantage plans eliminate Medigap premiums but create out-of-pocket risk through copays, coinsurance, and out-of-pocket maximums that can reach $8,000 or more annually per person, and the total annual cost varies dramatically based on how much healthcare we use. Someone who has a healthy year with just preventive care and a few doctor visits might pay only the Part B premium with no additional costs under their $0 premium Medicare Advantage plan, spending $2,096 annually, while someone who has surgery and complications might hit the $7,550 out-of-pocket maximum and spend $9,646 that year in total Medicare costs.

The Original Medicare with Medigap approach creates higher fixed costs through Medigap premiums but lower and more predictable out-of-pocket costs, and someone paying $200 monthly for Plan G plus $174.70 for Part B plus $35 for Part D spends $4,916 annually plus the $240 Part B deductible for total of $5,156, and this amount stays roughly the same whether they use minimal healthcare or have major medical events. The predictability appeals to people who want to budget fixed healthcare costs and not worry about variable expenses, while the lower base cost of Medicare Advantage appeals to people willing to accept risk of higher costs in exchange for saving $3,000 annually in years when they're healthy.

The provider access differences between Medicare Advantage networks and Original Medicare's universal acceptance create quality-of-life considerations beyond just cost, and someone who wants to see specialists at major medical centers or who travels extensively and wants healthcare access anywhere in the country strongly prefers Original Medicare. A couple spending several months per year in different states or traveling internationally can see any Medicare-accepting provider anywhere without worrying about networks or prior authorization, while someone in Medicare Advantage either needs to return to their network area for care or pay out-of-network costs that might not count toward their out-of-pocket maximum.

The dental and vision coverage that many Medicare Advantage plans include provides value that Original Medicare doesn't offer even with Medigap, and someone who needs glasses and dental work annually might save $800-1,200 through included benefits in their Advantage plan. Original Medicare covers essentially no routine dental care and no routine vision care, requiring separate dental insurance that costs $30-60 monthly and separate vision insurance or out-of-pocket payment for exams and glasses, and adding these to Medigap premiums increases the total cost advantage of Original Medicare over Advantage.

Part D plan selection requires comparing total annual cost including premiums and out-of-pocket drug costs rather than just looking at monthly premium, and the plan with the lowest premium often has the highest total cost for people taking expensive medications. Someone taking a medication that costs $500 monthly needs to check whether that drug is covered on each plan's formulary and what tier it's in, because one plan might have $40 monthly premium with the drug in tier 2 costing $80 copay while another plan has $60 monthly premium with the drug in tier 1 costing $15 copay, making the higher-premium plan $720 cheaper annually.

The Medicare Plan Finder tool on medicare.gov lets us enter all our medications and compare total annual costs across available Part D plans in our area, accounting for premiums, deductibles, and copays specific to our drugs. Someone taking five maintenance medications can get personalized cost estimates showing that Plan A costs $2,400 annually total while Plan B costs $1,800 despite having slightly higher premium, and using this tool during annual enrollment saves hundreds to thousands annually compared to just choosing the plan with the lowest premium or staying in the same plan without comparing alternatives.

The doughnut hole or coverage gap in Part D has been largely eliminated through gradual reforms, and starting in 2024 the gap no longer exists, with beneficiaries paying 25% coinsurance throughout the year until reaching catastrophic coverage. Someone taking expensive drugs benefits from gap elimination because they no longer face the spike in costs that occurred when entering the gap, and the predictable 25% coinsurance makes budgeting easier than the old system where costs jumped dramatically in the middle of the year before dropping again at catastrophic coverage.

Catastrophic coverage begins after we've spent $8,000 out-of-pocket in 2024, including our payments plus manufacturer discounts but not premiums, and after hitting this threshold we pay minimal copays of $4-10 per prescription for the rest of the year. Someone taking $15,000 annually in medications pays roughly 25% until hitting the catastrophic threshold, spending about $4,000 out-of-pocket to reach catastrophic coverage plus perhaps $600 in premiums, and then pays less than $100 for the remaining months, for total annual cost around $4,700 instead of the $3,750 they would pay without the catastrophic protection.

The low-income subsidies through Extra Help can eliminate Part D costs entirely for people who qualify, and the income limits of roughly $23,000 single or $31,000 married are higher than Medicaid limits but still exclude most retirees with even modest investment income or pensions. Someone with $22,000 in Social Security and pension income who qualifies for Extra Help pays no Part D premium, no deductible, and $4-10 copays per prescription regardless of drug cost, potentially saving $3,000-5,000 annually compared to unsubsidized Part D costs for someone taking expensive medications.

The asset limits for Extra Help of roughly $16,000 single or $32,000 married exclude retirement accounts, home value, and one vehicle, making qualification possible for some people with substantial home equity or retirement savings who have low current income. Someone with a $300,000 house and $200,000 in retirement accounts generating only $15,000 annually might qualify for Extra Help despite having significant net worth, because the house and retirement accounts don't count toward the asset test, and their low income from minimal withdrawals or Roth-heavy portfolio creates eligibility.

Spousal coverage considerations affect Medicare planning because each spouse enrolls separately and makes independent decisions about Advantage versus Original Medicare, though coordinating decisions often makes sense for couples. A couple might both choose Original Medicare with Medigap for consistent coverage and provider access, or both choose Medicare Advantage to minimize premiums, or they might split with one in Advantage and one in Original Medicare if their health status and preferences differ substantially. Someone with chronic conditions who sees specialists frequently might choose Original Medicare while their healthy spouse chooses Advantage, creating household Medicare costs of perhaps $7,000 annually instead of $10,000 if both chose Original Medicare or potential out-of-pocket costs of $15,000 if both chose Advantage and both hit high medical expenses.

The Medicare enrollment penalties for late Part B enrollment are 10% per 12-month period we should have had Part B but didn't, and these penalties last for as long as we have Part B coverage, effectively forever. Someone who delays Part B enrollment by three years without creditable employer coverage pays 30% penalty on top of base premium, turning $174.70 monthly into $227 monthly and wasting $628 annually forever, and over a 25-year retirement this totals $15,700 in unnecessary costs from missing the enrollment deadline.

Working past 65 with employer coverage requires careful attention to employer size and whether the coverage is creditable to avoid penalties while also avoiding unnecessary costs from dual coverage. Someone at a large employer with good coverage should probably delay Part B until they retire to avoid paying Part B premiums while still covered by employer plan, while someone at a small employer should enroll in Part B at 65 because the employer plan becomes secondary to Medicare and delaying Part B creates gaps in coverage and penalties. The confusion around these rules leads many people to make expensive mistakes, and checking with HR or Social Security before the initial enrollment deadline prevents problems.

The special enrollment period for people losing employer coverage gives eight months to enroll in Part B without penalty after the employer coverage ends, and understanding this window prevents gaps in coverage or missed deadlines. Someone who retires at 68 after working past 65 with employer coverage has eight months from retirement to enroll in Part B, and enrolling during this window avoids penalties and coverage gaps, while missing the eight-month deadline triggers late enrollment penalties and requires waiting for the next general enrollment period from January to March with coverage not starting until July.

The coordination of Medicare with retiree health coverage from former employers varies by employer, with some large employers offering generous retiree coverage that supplements Medicare and others offering minimal coverage or none at all. Someone whose former employer pays their Medigap premium or provides comprehensive supplemental coverage to Original Medicare might have total Medicare costs of only Part B and Part D premiums, while someone whose employer dropped all retiree coverage faces the full cost of premiums and out-of-pocket expenses. Understanding what retiree coverage is available before leaving employment helps with retirement planning, and the trend of employers reducing or eliminating retiree health benefits means fewer people can count on employer help with Medicare costs.

The Medicare tax on high earners adds 0.9% to wages and self-employment income above $200,000 single or $250,000 married, and while this doesn't directly affect benefit eligibility or costs, it represents additional Medicare-related taxation during working years. Someone earning $300,000 pays the standard 1.45% Medicare tax on all earnings plus an additional 0.9% on the $100,000 above $200,000, adding $900 to their annual tax bill, and this Additional Medicare Tax applies to individuals without the wage base cap that limits Social Security taxes.

The net investment income tax of 3.8% on investment income for people with MAGI above $200,000 single or $250,000 married was enacted alongside the Affordable Care Act and its revenue goes to Medicare, creating another form of Medicare-related taxation on high earners. Someone with $50,000 in investment income and MAGI of $230,000 pays 3.8% on the $30,000 above $200,000, adding $1,140 to their tax bill, and this tax applies to capital gains, dividends, interest, rental income, and other investment income but not to retirement account distributions that count as ordinary income rather than investment income.

The total Medicare costs for a healthy 65-year-old couple in 2024 choosing Original Medicare might be $10,000-12,000 annually including Part B premiums for both, Medigap Plan G for both, Part D for both, and the Part B deductibles, while the same couple choosing Medicare Advantage might pay $4,200 annually in base costs with potential out-of-pocket expenses up to $15,000 in a bad year but more likely $5,000-8,000 in typical years. By age 75 with IRMAA surcharges from RMDs and higher Medigap premiums due to age-based pricing, the Original Medicare couple might pay $14,000-16,000 annually, and by age 85 with even higher premiums and out-of-pocket costs, annual Medicare expenses might reach $18,000-20,000 per person even with good Medigap coverage.

Healthcare costs are one piece of retirement cash flow. How we pull money from different accounts to cover all of our costs — healthcare, housing, food, travel, everything — has its own logic. The order in which we tap different accounts affects taxes, subsidies, Medicare costs, and how long the money lasts. Getting this wrong is one of the most expensive and most avoidable retirement mistakes.

Which Account to Empty First

The order in which we withdraw from different account types affects lifetime taxes, Medicare premiums, Social Security taxation, ACA subsidies, and total wealth available over retirement, and optimizing this sequence can save tens of thousands to hundreds of thousands of dollars compared to naive approaches that ignore the tax implications of withdrawal choices. Someone with $500,000 in Traditional IRA, $300,000 in Roth IRA, and $200,000 in taxable accounts faces different tax consequences depending on which accounts they tap first, and the conventional wisdom of taking taxable first, then Traditional, then Roth last doesn't always produce the best outcome when we account for the full complexity of the tax code and means-tested benefits.

The taxable account first approach makes intuitive sense because these accounts don't have tax advantages we'd be wasting by withdrawing early, and taking from taxable accounts lets tax-advantaged accounts continue growing tax-deferred or tax-free for longer periods. Someone who spends down their $200,000 taxable account over five years while letting their $800,000 in retirement accounts grow sees the retirement accounts potentially reach $900,000 or more by the time they start withdrawing, and the deferral creates extra growth that wouldn't happen if they took from retirement accounts earlier. The challenge is that delaying Traditional IRA withdrawals until RMDs start at 73 can create large forced distributions that push us into high tax brackets and trigger IRMAA surcharges.

The specific identification of lots in taxable accounts lets us choose which shares to sell to minimize or maximize capital gains depending on our tax situation in a given year, and someone who bought stocks at different times with different cost bases can sell the high-basis shares to generate small gains or the low-basis shares to generate large gains. A person who bought $20,000 of stock in 2010 now worth $60,000 and bought $30,000 in 2020 now worth $35,000 can sell the 2020 shares showing only $5,000 in gains, or sell the 2010 shares showing $40,000 in gains, depending on whether they want to stay under the 0% capital gains threshold or they have losses to offset or they're in a year with low income where gains won't cost much in taxes.

The 0% long-term capital gains bracket for people with taxable income below roughly $47,000 single or $94,000 married creates opportunities to harvest gains tax-free during early retirement years when we're living on savings without much taxable income, and someone retiring at 60 with substantial unrealized gains in taxable accounts can sell appreciated positions each year while staying under the threshold, resetting basis higher and reducing future tax liability. A couple with $400,000 in taxable accounts showing $200,000 in unrealized gains can harvest $40,000-50,000 in gains annually from 60-65 while keeping total taxable income below $94,000, potentially eliminating all capital gains taxes on the entire account over those five years.

The Traditional IRA withdrawal timing involves balancing current tax costs against future RMD sizes and the tax rates those RMDs might trigger, and someone who waits until RMDs start at 73 might face forced distributions of $50,000 or more that push them into 22% or 24% brackets, while taking partial distributions earlier in retirement when income is low might keep them in the 12% bracket. A person with $800,000 in Traditional IRA at 65 faces RMDs of roughly $32,000 at 73, and if they have Social Security of $30,000 and no other income, the RMD pushes their total income to $62,000, putting some of it in the 22% bracket and causing 85% of Social Security to become taxable, creating marginal rates above 30% when accounting for the Social Security taxation torpedo.

The Roth conversion strategy during early retirement fills up lower tax brackets by converting Traditional IRA money to Roth before RMDs begin, and someone who converts $30,000 annually from Traditional to Roth from ages 65-72 moves $240,000 out of Traditional IRA, reducing the RMD base and lowering future forced distributions. The converted amount gets taxed in the conversion year at whatever bracket applies, potentially 12% or 22%, while the money then grows tax-free in Roth and never faces taxation again, and the reduced Traditional IRA balance creates lower RMDs that might keep future income in lower brackets, saving 10-20% in marginal tax rates on the reduced RMD amounts.

The breakeven analysis for Roth conversions compares the taxes paid on conversion today against the taxes saved on future RMDs, and someone paying 12% to convert $30,000 spends $3,600 in current taxes to avoid potentially 22% or more on that money plus growth in the future. If the $30,000 grows to $45,000 by the time RMDs would have started and staying in Traditional IRA would have taxed it at 22%, the future tax would be $9,900, saving $6,300 by converting early and paying only $3,600. The analysis gets more complex when accounting for IRMAA, Social Security taxation, and state taxes, but the general principle is that converting in low-bracket years to avoid high-bracket years in the future tends to work out favorably.

The ACA subsidy years from 60-65 create strong incentives to minimize MAGI by living on Roth withdrawals and taxable account principal rather than Traditional IRA withdrawals that show up as MAGI and reduce subsidies. Someone with MAGI of $40,000 receives substantial ACA subsidies that might be worth $10,000 annually, while MAGI of $70,000 might eliminate subsidies and require paying full premiums of $15,000-20,000, making the marginal cost of the extra $30,000 in MAGI potentially $25,000 or more when accounting for lost subsidies. This argues for aggressive Roth conversions in the years before 60, building up Roth balances that can be withdrawn during the ACA years without affecting subsidy eligibility.

The sequence for someone retiring at 60 might involve living on taxable account withdrawals plus Roth principal withdrawals from 60-65 to keep MAGI low for ACA subsidies, showing maybe $20,000-30,000 in MAGI while actually spending $50,000-60,000 annually, then at 65 when Medicare begins and subsidies no longer matter, starting to take Traditional IRA distributions to fill up lower brackets before RMDs begin at 73. Someone following this sequence might pay $3,000 annually for ACA coverage with subsidies instead of $18,000 full-price, saving $75,000 over five years, then pay modest taxes on Traditional IRA withdrawals from 65-72 instead of large taxes on RMDs from 73 onward.

The Social Security claiming decision interacts with withdrawal sequencing because claiming Social Security early adds taxable income that affects tax brackets and the taxation of Social Security itself, while delaying Social Security allows more Traditional IRA withdrawals or Roth conversions before Social Security income starts. Someone who claims Social Security at 62 showing $24,000 in benefits has less room for Traditional IRA withdrawals before hitting higher brackets, while someone who delays to 70 can do eight years of Roth conversions or Traditional IRA withdrawals from 62-70 without Social Security income affecting the calculation, potentially converting $240,000-300,000 to Roth during that window.

The taxation of Social Security benefits based on combined income creates a zone where withdrawing more from Traditional IRA causes not just the withdrawal to be taxed but also makes more Social Security taxable, effectively increasing marginal tax rates by 50-85% in the torpedo zone where benefits are phasing into taxation. Someone with $30,000 in Social Security and $20,000 in Traditional IRA withdrawals might have none of their Social Security taxable, while increasing Traditional IRA withdrawals to $40,000 might make $17,000 of Social Security taxable, creating $37,000 in taxable income instead of $20,000 from a $20,000 increase in withdrawals. This 1.85 multiplier effect makes Traditional IRA withdrawals very expensive in the Social Security taxation phase-in range.

The widow or widower situation changes withdrawal sequencing because when one spouse dies, household income drops substantially but tax brackets change from married to single, creating situations where the surviving spouse faces higher tax rates on the same income level. A couple living on $60,000 from Traditional IRA withdrawals pays taxes in the 12% bracket, but when one spouse dies and the survivor continues taking $60,000 in withdrawals, they're now filing as single and much of that income falls into the 22% bracket, effectively raising taxes by 10% on a substantial portion of income without any increase in actual income or standard of living.

The beneficiary planning for Traditional IRA versus Roth IRA creates different tax outcomes for heirs, and someone who converts Traditional IRA to Roth pays taxes now at their own rates but leaves heirs Roth accounts that distribute tax-free, versus leaving Traditional IRA that forces heirs to pay taxes at their potentially higher rates. A person converting $300,000 from Traditional to Roth over several years paying effective rate of 15% spends $45,000 in taxes but leaves heirs $255,000 in Roth that distributes with no tax consequences, while leaving $300,000 in Traditional IRA creates $300,000 of taxable distributions for heirs who might pay 24% or 32% depending on their income, costing them $72,000-96,000 in taxes.

The 10-year distribution requirement for inherited IRAs under the SECURE Act means non-spouse beneficiaries must withdraw the entire inherited IRA within 10 years, and if the inherited account is Traditional IRA, this creates bunched income that might push heirs into high brackets. Someone inheriting $500,000 Traditional IRA at age 45 while earning $100,000 annually faces taking $50,000 per year in IRA distributions on top of their salary, pushing them into 32% or 35% brackets on the IRA distributions and potentially losing some to NIIT as well, while inheriting $500,000 in Roth creates the same distribution requirement but no tax consequences.

The state tax considerations affect withdrawal sequencing for people living in high-tax states during some retirement years and low-tax or no-tax states during others, and someone who spends winters in Florida but is technically a New York resident might want to establish Florida residency before doing large Traditional IRA withdrawals or Roth conversions to avoid New York's 6-10% state income tax. The timing of a move from California to Nevada or Texas can save tens of thousands in state taxes on Traditional IRA distributions, and someone with $600,000 to withdraw over retirement saves roughly $36,000-60,000 by being a resident of a no-income-tax state versus California at 6-10% rates.

The charitable contributions through Qualified Charitable Distributions from IRA starting at age 70.5 provide a way to satisfy RMDs without increasing taxable income, and someone who donates $10,000 annually to charity can make those donations directly from their IRA, reducing their RMD requirement and avoiding income tax on the donated amount. A person with RMD of $35,000 who makes $10,000 QCD shows only $25,000 in taxable income from the IRA instead of $35,000, saving taxes at their marginal rate plus potentially avoiding IRMAA or Social Security taxation torpedo effects, making the QCD worth 30-40% more than donating cash after paying tax on the RMD.

The standard deduction for people 65 and older increases by $1,950 per person in 2024, providing $29,200 for single filers and $30,700 for married filing jointly, and this creates room to withdraw from Traditional IRA without paying federal income tax up to these amounts. A married couple both over 65 can take $30,700 from Traditional IRA and owe no federal income tax because the standard deduction eliminates the taxable income, making Traditional IRA withdrawals up to this amount effectively tax-free, though state taxes and the interaction with Social Security taxation might reduce the benefit.

The Roth conversion ladder for early retirees involves converting amounts from Traditional to Roth and then waiting five years before withdrawing the converted amounts, creating a pipeline of money that becomes accessible without penalty. Someone retiring at 55 can convert $40,000 from Traditional to Roth each year from 55-59, paying taxes on the conversions, and then starting at 60 they can withdraw the first year's conversion penalty-free because five years have passed, continuing each subsequent year to access conversions from five years prior. This creates penalty-free access to retirement money before 59.5 without needing to use 72(t) substantially equal periodic payments.

The substantially equal periodic payment option under 72(t) allows penalty-free withdrawals from IRA before 59.5 if we commit to taking calculated amounts for at least five years or until 59.5, whichever is longer, and the payments get calculated using IRS-approved methods based on life expectancy and account balance. Someone who is 52 with $400,000 in IRA might calculate payments of roughly $15,000 annually under the RMD method, taking this amount each year until 59.5 without penalty, but if they modify the payments or stop before the required period ends, all the previous years' penalty exceptions get retroactively revoked and they owe penalties plus interest on every withdrawal.

The flexibility of withdrawal sequencing decreases once RMDs begin because we must take the minimum required distribution before doing anything else with Traditional IRA money, and someone who wanted to do a $50,000 Roth conversion at 75 must first satisfy their $40,000 RMD, meaning they're taking $90,000 from Traditional IRA that year with the corresponding tax consequences. The RMD requirement limits optimization opportunities after 73, which is why the years from retirement until RMDs begin represent the most valuable window for tax planning through Roth conversions, Roth IRA withdrawals, and strategic Traditional IRA distributions.

The net investment income tax of 3.8% applies to investment income including capital gains and dividends when MAGI exceeds $200,000 single or $250,000 married, and withdrawal sequencing can affect whether we exceed these thresholds and face the surcharge. Someone with $180,000 in Social Security and Traditional IRA withdrawals who sells stock showing $80,000 in capital gains pushes their MAGI to $260,000 and pays NIIT on $10,000 of investment income, while if they had done Roth conversions in earlier years and could take $100,000 from Roth plus $80,000 in capital gains, they'd show MAGI of only $80,000 and avoid NIIT entirely.

The alternative minimum tax rarely affects retirees but can trigger in years with large Roth conversions combined with significant capital gains and certain deductions, and someone doing a $100,000 Roth conversion in a year when they also have $60,000 in capital gains might find that AMT applies, effectively limiting their ability to use certain deductions and credits. The AMT calculation is complex enough that major financial moves like large conversions or exercising stock options warrant running the numbers through tax software to see whether AMT kicks in and reduces the benefit of the transaction.

The overall strategy for withdrawal sequencing involves using taxable accounts during ACA subsidy years while minimizing MAGI, doing Roth conversions in low-income years before RMDs begin to reduce future tax burden, harvesting capital gains at 0% rate when possible, coordinating Social Security claiming with Traditional IRA withdrawals to minimize the taxation torpedo, using QCDs for charitable giving after 70.5, and generally thinking across the entire retirement timeline rather than optimizing any single year in isolation. Someone who executes this well might pay 10-15% effective tax rate on retirement income, while someone who ignores sequencing and just withdraws randomly from different accounts might pay 20-25% on similar income, costing $50,000-100,000 over a 30-year retirement.

Withdrawal sequencing optimizes income from existing assets. Geography can change how much income we need in the first place. The difference in total retirement spending between an expensive city and a cheap one is large enough that location choice affects how much we need to save more than almost any other single variable.

Cheaper by Design

Housing costs vary by a factor of three to five between expensive coastal cities and affordable inland areas, and someone paying $3,000 per month for a modest house in San Francisco or Boston could buy a comparable or better house for $1,000 per month in Pensacola or Tulsa, saving $24,000 annually on housing alone before accounting for differences in property taxes, insurance, and utilities. This $24,000 annual savings reduces the portfolio size needed for retirement by $600,000 at a 4% withdrawal rate, meaning someone who can afford to retire with $1.2 million in an expensive city could retire with $600,000 in a cheap city while maintaining the same lifestyle, effectively buying themselves 10-15 more years of portfolio accumulation time.

The state income tax differential adds another layer of savings because moving from California with 9.3% state tax on middle incomes or New York with 6.5% to Florida or Texas with zero state income tax saves thousands to tens of thousands annually depending on retirement income. Someone with $80,000 in annual retirement income from Traditional IRA withdrawals, Social Security, and pension pays roughly $5,600 in California state income tax or $4,200 in New York tax, while paying zero in Florida or Texas, and over 30 years of retirement this difference totals $130,000-170,000 in state taxes paid versus not paid for making an identical income in different locations.

Property taxes create the opposite pattern where some low-cost-of-living states like Texas and New Hampshire charge high property tax rates of 1.5-2% of home value while high-cost states like California cap property taxes at 1% through Proposition 13, and someone with a $300,000 house pays $3,000 annually in California versus $5,000 in Texas. The total tax burden combines income and property taxes, and a retiree with $300,000 house and $80,000 income pays $8,600 annually in California versus $5,000 in Texas despite the property tax differential, because the zero income tax in Texas outweighs the higher property tax, saving $3,600 annually or $108,000 over 30 years.

Healthcare costs before 65 vary dramatically by location through ACA marketplace pricing, and identical coverage for a 60-year-old might cost $800 per month in Florida versus $1,400 per month in Alaska or Wyoming, creating $7,200 annual savings from living in a lower-cost healthcare market. Someone planning early retirement needs to research ACA premiums in potential target locations before committing to a move, because the healthcare savings or costs can equal or exceed housing savings in some cases, particularly for people in their late 50s and early 60s when age-based premiums are highest.

The sales tax rates and structures create less dramatic differences than income taxes but still matter over decades of spending, and someone spending $40,000 annually on taxable goods faces $2,800 in sales taxes in Tennessee at 7% average rate versus $0 in Oregon with no sales tax, though Oregon has state income tax that Tennessee lacks. The total tax burden calculation needs to account for all tax types rather than focusing on any single component, and someone who avoids state income tax by moving to Washington but then pays 10% sales tax on most purchases might not save as much as expected compared to living in a low-income-tax state with lower sales taxes.

The cost of living indices published by various organizations attempt to quantify total cost differences between cities, and these show that living in Manhattan costs roughly 170% of the national average while living in rural Alabama costs about 75% of the national average, implying someone who needs $60,000 to live adequately in Alabama needs $136,000 to maintain the same lifestyle in Manhattan. These indices aggregate housing, food, transportation, healthcare, and other costs into overall measures, though individual circumstances vary and someone who owns their home outright might find smaller cost-of-living differences than someone who rents.

The lifestyle quality trade-offs between expensive and cheap locations involve subjective factors like cultural amenities, climate, proximity to family and friends, and community fit that can't be reduced to dollar values. Someone moving from Seattle to Jacksonville saves $25,000 annually but gives up the Pacific Northwest climate, the cultural scene they're accustomed to, and proximity to long-time friends, and whether this trade is worth making depends on personal values and priorities that vary enormously between individuals. The purely financial calculation says move to the cheapest viable location, while the life satisfaction calculation might say stay where social connections and preferred lifestyle exist even if it costs significantly more.

The proximity to family considerations create constraints on geographic flexibility because many people want to live near children or grandchildren or aging parents who need support, and if family lives in expensive locations, the financial pressure to move elsewhere conflicts with the desire to maintain close family connections. Someone whose children live in the Bay Area faces either paying high costs to live near grandchildren or saving money by living elsewhere but only seeing grandchildren a few times per year, and some people prioritize family proximity highly enough to accept the financial burden while others prioritize financial security and accept the distance.

The timing of moves can optimize for both financial and personal factors by spending high-earning working years in expensive cities where jobs and salaries are highest, then moving to cheaper locations upon retirement when income needs drop and geographic flexibility increases. Someone who works in New York City until 60 earning $150,000 and then retires to North Carolina gets the benefits of high salary during accumulation years and low costs during distribution years, though the transition requires leaving behind social networks built over decades of living in one place.

The international arbitrage involves moving to countries with much lower costs of living than the United States, and places like Mexico, Portugal, Ecuador, or Thailand offer high-quality housing and lifestyle for $2,000-3,000 per month total expenses that would cost $5,000-7,000 in the U.S. Someone with $400,000 saved who couldn't retire in the U.S. because the 4% rule only provides $16,000 annually could retire comfortably in these lower-cost countries on that amount, effectively buying themselves retirement 10-15 years earlier than possible domestically.

The healthcare access in international locations varies from excellent and inexpensive in places like Mexico and Thailand where high-quality medical care costs a fraction of U.S. prices, to questionable or limited in more remote or less developed areas. Someone retiring to Mexico can get quality healthcare for cash prices that are 50-70% lower than U.S. prices even without insurance, and international health insurance plans cost $100-200 monthly versus $800-1,200 for comparable U.S. coverage, creating healthcare savings of $8,000-13,000 annually beyond the obvious housing and cost-of-living savings.

The Medicare complications of living abroad mean we can't use Medicare coverage outside the U.S. except in limited circumstances near borders, and someone who moves internationally before 65 should plan to stay until 65 or return periodically for healthcare, while someone who moves after 65 either needs to return to the U.S. for care, pay cash locally, or maintain international insurance for non-Medicare-covered services. The strategy of living abroad from 60-65 and then returning to the U.S. at 65 for Medicare eligibility gives five years of very low costs during early retirement and then brings us back for the senior years when healthcare needs typically increase.

The visa and residency requirements for international retirement vary by country, with some offering specific retirement visas that grant residency based on proving minimum income or savings, typically $1,000-2,000 monthly income or $30,000-50,000 in savings. Mexico, Panama, Portugal, and Ecuador all offer relatively accessible retirement visa programs, while other countries make it much harder to obtain long-term residency, and research into specific visa requirements before committing to an international move prevents discovering too late that we can't legally stay long-term.

The cultural and language barriers create challenges that some people navigate easily and others find overwhelming, and someone who speaks Spanish fluently and enjoys immersion in new cultures might thrive in Mexico or Ecuador, while someone who struggles with languages and prefers familiar cultural patterns might be miserable despite the financial benefits. The lower costs only create value if we can actually live in and enjoy the location, and someone who is lonely and isolated in a cheap foreign city might prefer spending more to live in a familiar U.S. community where they have social connections.

The property ownership in foreign countries involves different legal systems and potential risks including less robust property rights, more corruption, and difficulties enforcing contracts or recovering property in disputes. Someone who buys property in Mexico or Central America faces scenarios where title might be contested, where local officials might demand bribes for permits or services, or where property could be seized or devalued through government action, creating risks that don't exist to the same degree in U.S. property ownership. Renting rather than buying in international locations reduces this risk but eliminates the potential for building home equity.

The currency risk affects international retirement because most of our savings are in dollars but our expenses are in the local currency, and exchange rate movements can substantially increase or decrease the local currency value of our dollar income. Someone with $30,000 annual budget who moves to Mexico when the exchange rate is 20 pesos per dollar has 600,000 pesos to spend, but if the peso strengthens to 15 per dollar, their 600,000 pesos now costs $40,000, effectively reducing their purchasing power by 25% through currency movement alone. The reverse can also happen where dollar strengthens and our purchasing power increases, but the volatility creates uncertainty in financial planning.

The Social Security payments continue when living abroad in most countries, and someone receiving $2,000 monthly in Social Security benefits can have those deposited in a U.S. bank and then transfer what's needed to local accounts, maintaining the reliable dollar-denominated income stream while living elsewhere. A few countries face payment restrictions or prohibitions, but major retirement destinations like Mexico, Portugal, and Thailand all allow Social Security payments to continue uninterrupted, making them viable for people whose retirement income is heavily dependent on Social Security.

The tax obligations follow U.S. citizens everywhere in the world, requiring continued filing of U.S. tax returns on worldwide income and potentially paying U.S. taxes even while living abroad, though foreign earned income exclusions and foreign tax credits reduce or eliminate most tax obligations for people living on retirement income rather than continuing to work. Someone with $60,000 in retirement income from Social Security and IRA withdrawals files U.S. tax returns showing this income and pays U.S. taxes on it regardless of where they live, while someone who takes a job in Portugal and earns foreign income can exclude up to $120,000 of foreign earned income from U.S. taxation.

The repatriation planning matters because someone who moves abroad at 60 might want or need to return to the U.S. at 75 or 80 when health declines or when they want to be near family, and maintaining residency status in a preferred U.S. state or city might require periodic returns or maintaining a property, while giving up U.S. residency entirely and then trying to return late in life creates complications. The strategy of maintaining a small property in a low-cost U.S. state as a home base while living primarily abroad provides flexibility to return easily if circumstances change, though it adds costs during the international years.

The domestic geographic arbitrage through snowbirding involves maintaining residences in two locations and moving seasonally to optimize weather and costs, and someone who owns a house in Michigan but rents in Arizona for November through March gets favorable Michigan costs for most of the year plus Arizona winter weather while declaring Michigan residency for tax purposes if Michigan has lower taxes than Arizona. The dual-location approach costs more than living in one cheap place year-round but provides weather optimization and lifestyle variation that some people value enough to accept the higher costs.

The residency determination for state tax purposes depends on factors including where we spend most of our time, where we're registered to vote, where our driver's license is from, and where we claim homestead exemption, and someone who maintains addresses in multiple states needs to clearly establish residency in the preferred state to avoid being taxed by the higher-tax state. The residency rules vary by state and disputes can arise when multiple states claim us as residents, making clean establishment of residency through clustering all indicators in one state the safest approach rather than having split indicators across states.

The social isolation risk in geographic arbitrage particularly affects single retirees who move away from established social networks to cheaper locations and then struggle to build new connections in their 60s or 70s, and someone who moves to a retirement community in Florida might make new friends relatively easily through structured activities, while someone who moves to rural Montana where they know no one might end up lonely and isolated despite the cost savings. The importance of social connection to health and longevity suggests that pure financial optimization without considering social factors can backfire if we end up depressed and isolated in a cheap location.

The medical specialist access varies dramatically between major metro areas with comprehensive academic medical centers and small towns or rural areas where even basic specialists might be hours away, and someone with complex health conditions requiring oncologists, cardiologists, or other specialists needs access to quality care that might not exist in the cheapest locations. The trade-off between costs and healthcare access matters more as we age and health issues become more likely, and someone healthy at 60 who moves to a remote cheap location might regret the decision at 75 when they develop conditions requiring frequent specialist visits.

The quality of life factors including air quality, climate, crime rates, walkability, and cultural amenities create substantial variation in desirability between locations at similar price points, and someone choosing between similarly affordable cities should research these quality factors rather than just picking the absolute cheapest option. A city with $1,200 monthly housing costs, good air quality, low crime, and walkable neighborhoods might provide better retirement satisfaction than a city with $900 monthly housing costs but high crime, pollution, and car-dependent sprawl, making the extra $300 monthly a worthwhile investment in quality of life.

The trial runs through extended visits or short-term rentals before committing to permanent relocation reduce the risk of discovering too late that a location doesn't fit our needs or preferences, and someone considering a move to Austin or Asheville should spend several months living there across different seasons before selling their current home and buying in the new location. The costs of moving are high enough that making a mistake and needing to move again wastes tens of thousands in moving costs, realtor commissions, and transaction fees, making it worth investing in thorough exploration before committing.

The overall strategy for geographic arbitrage involves calculating total costs including housing, taxes, healthcare, and other location-dependent expenses across potential target locations, weighing financial savings against quality-of-life factors and proximity to family, considering international options for those willing to accept more complexity and risk in exchange for much larger savings, and potentially timing moves to optimize for working years in expensive high-salary locations and retirement years in cheap low-cost locations. Someone who executes geographic arbitrage well might reduce required portfolio size by $300,000-600,000 or enable retirement 5-10 years earlier than possible by staying in an expensive location, though the benefits only accrue if the destination actually works for our lifestyle and we don't end up moving back after a few unhappy years.

Staying in a lower-cost location is one way to reduce the gap between income and expenses. Working part-time is another. For people who retire before 65, or who retire with portfolios that are adequate but not cushioned, part-time work in the first decade of retirement is one of the most effective risk reduction tools available — and one of the most underused.

Working Because You Want To

Working part-time during retirement can reduce or eliminate the need to withdraw from investment portfolios during vulnerable early years when sequence of returns risk is highest, and someone earning $20,000 annually from part-time work while spending $50,000 only needs to withdraw $30,000 from their portfolio instead of $50,000, reducing sequence risk by 40% and substantially improving portfolio survival rates. The psychological transition from full-time career to complete retirement can be jarring for people whose identity and social connections are tied to work, and part-time employment provides a gentler glide path that maintains some work identity and structure while freeing up time for leisure activities and travel.

The earnings test for Social Security before full retirement age creates a disincentive to work while claiming benefits early, because earning more than roughly $22,320 in 2024 results in $1 of benefits withheld for every $2 earned above the limit, effectively creating a 50% marginal tax on earnings. Someone claiming Social Security at 62 while earning $40,000 per year loses $8,840 in Social Security benefits to the earnings test, and when combined with income taxes and payroll taxes, the effective marginal rate on those earnings approaches 70-80%, making part-time work while claiming Social Security early economically unwise for most people.

The earnings test disappears at full retirement age, so someone who reaches 67 can earn unlimited amounts without any reduction in Social Security benefits, making part-time work at or after full retirement age much more attractive than working while claiming early. Someone who delays Social Security claiming until 67 or 70 can work part-time during the interim years without facing the earnings test penalty, taking advantage of delayed retirement credits that increase their eventual benefit by 8% per year while also earning income that reduces portfolio withdrawals and potentially allows additional retirement savings.

The health insurance costs for early retirees working part-time depend on whether the employer offers coverage, and someone working 30 hours per week at a company that provides health benefits to part-timers can get employer coverage that might cost $200-400 monthly in employee premiums instead of $800-1,200 monthly for individual ACA coverage, saving $7,200-12,000 annually. Jobs at Starbucks, Costco, UPS, and some other large employers famously offer health benefits to part-time workers at 20-30 hours per week, creating opportunities to bridge the gap from early retirement to Medicare at 65 while maintaining health coverage.

The flexibility of part-time work appeals to retirees who want to travel or pursue hobbies because they can choose seasonal work, project-based consulting, or variable hour arrangements that don't require year-round commitment, and someone who works as a tax preparer from January to April earning $15,000 has eight months free to travel while still generating income that reduces annual portfolio withdrawals. The control over schedule that many part-time roles provide creates better work-life balance than full-time career employment, and someone who spent their career responding to emails at all hours and attending endless meetings might find part-time work on their own terms genuinely enjoyable rather than just financially necessary.

Consulting or freelancing using career skills can generate high hourly rates that make it possible to earn substantial income while working relatively few hours, and someone who spent their career as an accountant, engineer, or project manager might bill at $100-150 per hour for 10-15 hours per week, generating $50,000-100,000 annually while maintaining significant free time. The challenge is building a client base and dealing with irregular income and lack of benefits, but for people with in-demand skills and professional networks, consulting can provide the ideal combination of income and flexibility.

The seasonal work opportunities in retail, tourism, tax preparation, and agriculture allow people to earn concentrated income during peak seasons and then have extended time off, and someone who works retail during the November-December holiday season earning $8,000 or someone who works at a national park from May-September earning $15,000 can cover a meaningful portion of annual expenses while having most of the year free.

The downside is that seasonal work often pays relatively low hourly rates and can be physically demanding, making it more suitable for healthy retirees in their early 60s than for people in their 70s or those with physical limitations.

The gig economy platforms including ride-sharing, delivery services, and task-based work through apps provide maximum flexibility where we can work exactly when we want without any schedule commitment, and someone who drives for Uber on Friday and Saturday nights earning $300 per weekend brings in $15,600 annually while working only two days per week and maintaining complete control over when they work. The drawbacks include vehicle wear and tear, lack of benefits, and earnings that might be below minimum wage after accounting for expenses, plus the physical and mental demands of dealing with passengers or navigating unfamiliar areas.

The small business or side business that someone started during their working years can continue into retirement providing income without the demands of building a business from scratch, and someone who operated a photography business or rental property on the side while working full-time can continue that business in retirement while scaling hours to preference. The transition from side business to primary income source in retirement can work well because the business is already established with existing clients or revenue streams, avoiding the risk and startup phase that makes launching a new business in retirement challenging.

The teaching or adjunct work at community colleges or continuing education programs appeals to retirees with expertise in specific subjects who enjoy sharing knowledge, and someone who spent their career as an engineer or business professional might teach one or two courses per semester earning $3,000-5,000 per course while engaging with students and maintaining intellectual stimulation. The academic calendar provides built-in breaks during winter, spring, and summer when teaching obligations pause, allowing extended travel or leisure time, and the relatively light workload of teaching one or two courses leaves substantial free time during the semester.

The non-profit work or jobs at libraries, museums, or cultural institutions often provide meaningful work at modest pay levels that appeal to retirees who prioritize purpose and social contribution over maximizing income, and someone who works at a local museum or nature center earning $15 per hour for 20 hours per week generates $15,600 annually while feeling good about contributing to community institutions they value. The trade-off is accepting lower pay than other opportunities might offer, but for people with adequate retirement savings who want to work primarily for purpose rather than financial necessity, these roles can be ideal.

The caregiving work for elderly or disabled individuals through home health agencies pays $15-20 per hour and offers flexible scheduling, and someone who works as a home health aide or companion for 15-20 hours per week earns $12,000-20,000 annually while helping people who need assistance, creating a sense of purpose alongside the income. The emotional and physical demands of caregiving work make it unsuitable for everyone, and someone who finds this work draining rather than fulfilling should look for different part-time options even if the pay is comparable.

The bridge jobs between full-time career and complete retirement might involve taking a position at significantly lower pay and responsibility than our career job, and someone who was a corporate executive earning $200,000 might work as a project manager earning $60,000 for a few years while transitioning to retirement, accepting the pay cut in exchange for lower stress and better work-life balance. The challenge is psychological, as people accustomed to senior roles and high compensation might struggle with reduced status and authority, but for those who can let go of ego, bridge jobs provide a gradual off-ramp from intense career to leisure.

The phased retirement arrangements where we negotiate reduced hours or responsibilities with our existing employer can be ideal because we maintain health benefits, continue in familiar work with known colleagues, and gradually reduce work commitment rather than making a hard stop. Someone who negotiates to work three days per week or six months per year with their current employer gets the benefits of part-time work without having to find a new employer or build a freelance client base, though not all employers accommodate these arrangements and some organizational cultures make it difficult to work part-time in professional roles.

The income limits for Roth IRA contributions require earned income, so someone earning $20,000 from part-time work can contribute $7,000 to a Roth IRA assuming they're under the income phase-out thresholds, continuing to build tax-free retirement savings even while in retirement. This creates an interesting strategy where part-time work generates both current income that reduces portfolio withdrawals and additional retirement savings that increase portfolio balance, providing a double benefit that accelerates portfolio growth during early retirement years.

The marginal tax rate on part-time earnings can be quite high when accounting for federal and state income taxes, payroll taxes, potential Social Security taxation torpedo effects, and possible loss of ACA subsidies, making the effective marginal rate approach 50-60% or higher. Someone with $40,000 in retirement income from portfolio withdrawals who earns $20,000 from part-time work might see $10,000-12,000 disappear to various taxes, and if the additional income pushes them above ACA subsidy thresholds, they might lose another $5,000-8,000 in subsidies, leaving them with only $2,000-5,000 net benefit from $20,000 of work.

The portfolio withdrawal reduction from part-time work provides benefits beyond just the obvious reduction in sequence risk by allowing more aggressive portfolio allocations and higher expected returns, because someone who has $20,000 per year in part-time income covering basic expenses can invest their portfolio more aggressively knowing they're not dependent on it for near-term living expenses. Someone earning $25,000 from part-time work might maintain an 80% stock allocation while someone fully dependent on portfolio withdrawals might need 50% stocks to manage volatility, and over 10-15 years of part-time work this allocation difference might generate $100,000 or more in additional portfolio growth.

The Social Security benefit increases from additional years of work can boost lifetime Social Security income because each additional year of earnings potentially replaces a lower-earning year in the 35-year calculation, and someone who earned $30,000 early in their career and then works part-time earning $25,000 at age 65 might see a small benefit increase as the $25,000 year replaces an even lower year from the past. The increases are typically modest, perhaps $20-40 per month or $240-480 annually, but over a 25-year retirement this adds up to $6,000-12,000 in additional lifetime benefits.

The forced retirement from health problems, caregiving responsibilities, or job loss affects many people's ability to work part-time in retirement, and someone who plans to work until 70 but develops health problems at 66 that prevent work faces the reality that their plan doesn't align with circumstances. The planning for part-time work should include consideration of whether we have the health, skills, and opportunities to actually work if we want to, rather than assuming work will be available and we'll be able to do it, and having backup plans for scenarios where part-time work doesn't materialize becomes important.

The ageism in hiring creates real barriers to finding part-time work for people in their 60s and 70s, particularly in fields like technology where youth is valued and older workers face discrimination both overt and subtle. Someone who is 65 and applies for part-time jobs might find that employers prefer younger workers even for positions where experience should be an advantage, and the combination of age discrimination and overqualification concerns means that finding good part-time work can be harder than anticipated.

The meaning and purpose that work provides becomes more important as pure financial need decreases, and someone with adequate retirement savings who works part-time might be doing it primarily for social connection, intellectual stimulation, and sense of purpose rather than income, making job satisfaction and work environment more important than pay rate. The willingness to accept lower pay for more meaningful work or better work environment increases when we're not financially desperate, and someone who can afford to be selective might choose a museum job at $15 per hour over retail work at $18 per hour because they find the museum work more engaging and enjoyable.

The volunteer work as an alternative to paid part-time work provides many of the same benefits of purpose, social connection, and structure without the income, and someone who doesn't need the money but wants to stay active and engaged might find that volunteering 15 hours per week at a food bank or literacy program meets their needs better than paid work that comes with obligations and stress. The trade-off is foregoing income that could reduce portfolio withdrawals or fund additional discretionary spending, but for people with adequate resources who prioritize meaning over marginal income, volunteering might be the better choice.

The transition out of part-time work when we reach our mid-70s or when health declines requires planning for the reality that working into our 80s isn't likely for most people even if they enjoy it and want to continue, and someone who works part-time from 62-75 generating $20,000 annually needs to ensure their portfolio can handle full withdrawal needs starting at 75 when work income stops. The planning should account for a realistic work timeline rather than optimistically assuming we'll work as long as we want, and building portfolio balances that can sustain us whether we work until 75 or are forced to stop at 68 provides resilience against health problems or job loss.

The overall strategy for part-time work in retirement involves finding opportunities that provide adequate pay while maintaining flexibility and meaning, timing work to reduce portfolio withdrawals during vulnerable early retirement years when sequence risk is highest, avoiding work while claiming Social Security early if earnings will trigger the earnings test, considering whether employer health benefits are available and valuable, being realistic about age discrimination and health limitations that might prevent working as long as planned, and viewing part-time work as a tool that enhances retirement rather than as a sign of inadequate planning or failure, because someone who chooses to work part-time while retired can often have a more enjoyable and secure retirement than someone who stopped working entirely as soon as financially possible.

The financial plan is for our own lifetime. What happens to what's left after we're gone — who gets it, how they get it, and what they pay in taxes to receive it —

is a different set of questions that most people put off until they're in their 70s. Putting it off further doesn't make the questions go away; it makes the answers worse.

After You're Gone

Wills determine who receives our assets when we die and who has authority to manage the distribution process, and dying without a will means state intestacy laws decide who gets what based on formulas that might not match our preferences, typically giving everything to a spouse or dividing between spouse and children in proportions set by statute rather than by our intentions. Someone who dies without a will in a state where intestacy law gives half to the spouse and half to children creates complications if the spouse needs the full estate to maintain their lifestyle, and the children might legally own half the house or retirement accounts even though the surviving spouse is still alive and living in the house.

The executor named in the will handles paying debts, filing final tax returns, distributing assets to beneficiaries, and generally wrapping up the deceased person's financial affairs, and choosing someone reliable, organized, and willing to serve matters enormously because a poor executor can delay distributions for years and create conflict among beneficiaries. Someone who names their oldest child as executor but that child lives across the country and has a demanding job might find the estate administration dragging on because the executor doesn't have time to handle the required tasks, while naming a local sibling or trusted friend who is retired and detail-oriented might result in efficient administration that wraps up in months rather than years.

The probate process involves the court system validating the will and overseeing estate administration, and this process can take six months to two years depending on estate complexity and state procedures, during which assets are frozen and beneficiaries can't access their inheritance. Someone who dies with $800,000 in assets that go through probate might see their heirs waiting 12-18 months before receiving distributions, paying $15,000-40,000 in legal fees and court costs depending on the state and whether anyone contests the will, and dealing with the stress and complexity of court oversight throughout the process.

Avoiding probate through beneficiary designations, joint ownership, or trusts provides faster access to assets and lower costs, and someone who properly titles all major assets to transfer outside probate can leave heirs who receive everything within weeks of death rather than waiting over a year for court proceedings to complete. Retirement accounts with designated beneficiaries pass directly to those beneficiaries outside probate, and someone with $500,000 in IRA who names their spouse as beneficiary sees the spouse receive the IRA within days or weeks of providing a death certificate to the custodian, while $500,000 in a brokerage account without beneficiary designation or joint ownership goes through probate and takes months.

The beneficiary designations on retirement accounts, life insurance, and payable-on-death bank accounts supersede the will, and someone whose will says everything goes to their current spouse but whose IRA beneficiary designation still lists their ex-spouse from a marriage that ended 15 years ago will see the IRA go to the ex-spouse regardless of what the will says. Updating beneficiary designations after marriage, divorce, births, and deaths prevents unintended consequences where outdated designations send hundreds of thousands of dollars to people we no longer want to inherit, and reviewing designations every few years ensures they still match our current intentions.

The per stirpes versus per capita distinction in beneficiary designations determines what happens if a beneficiary dies before us, with per stirpes sending that beneficiary's share to their descendants while per capita redistributes to the surviving named beneficiaries. Someone who names three children as equal beneficiaries per stirpes and one child predeceases them sees that deceased child's share going to their own children, the grandchildren of the original account owner, while per capita designation would give the deceased child's share to the two surviving children instead of the grandchildren, and the choice depends on whether we want to include grandchildren as potential beneficiaries if our children die before us.

Revocable living trusts avoid probate by transferring asset ownership to the trust during our lifetime while we maintain complete control as trustee, and upon death the successor trustee distributes assets according to the trust document without court involvement, providing privacy, speed, and lower costs than probate. Someone who establishes a living trust and retitles their house, brokerage accounts, and other major assets into the trust name maintains full control during life but ensures these assets transfer quickly to beneficiaries after death, potentially saving $20,000-50,000 in probate costs and avoiding the 12-18 month probate timeline.

The trust administration after death still requires the successor trustee to pay debts, file tax returns, and distribute assets, but this happens privately without court oversight and moves faster than probate, and someone who dies with assets in a trust might see beneficiaries receiving distributions within 3-6 months versus 12-24 months for probate. The upfront cost of establishing a trust runs $1,500-3,000 for basic situations or $3,000-6,000 for complex estates, and the ongoing maintenance requires retitling assets and potentially updating the trust document when circumstances change, but for people with estates over $300,000 or complicated family situations, these costs often make sense compared to probate expenses and delays.

Power of attorney for finances designates someone to handle our financial affairs if we become incapacitated, and without this document, family members must go to court to get conservatorship or guardianship which takes months and costs thousands in legal fees. Someone who has a stroke at 68 and can't manage their finances needs their designated agent under power of attorney to pay bills, file taxes, manage investments, and handle other financial tasks, and having this authority in place before incapacity occurs prevents the family from facing immediate financial crisis when bills go unpaid because no one has legal authority to access accounts.

The healthcare power of attorney or healthcare proxy designates someone to make medical decisions when we can't make them ourselves, and this becomes critical during serious illness or injury when treatment decisions need to be made quickly and we're unconscious or incapacitated. Someone in a coma after an accident needs their designated healthcare agent to make decisions about surgery, medications, life support, and other treatments, and without this designation, doctors might turn to next-of-kin based on state law which might not be the person we'd want making these decisions.

Living wills or advance directives specify our preferences for end-of-life care including whether we want life support, artificial nutrition and hydration, and aggressive interventions when we're terminally ill or in permanent vegetative state, and these documents guide healthcare agents and medical providers in honoring our wishes when we can't communicate them. Someone who would not want to be kept alive by machines if they're brain-dead with no chance of recovery can document this preference in a living will, helping their family avoid the agonizing decision of whether to withdraw life support by making clear that this is what we would want.

The HIPAA authorization allows designated people to access our medical information and communicate with healthcare providers, and without this authorization, doctors and hospitals can't share information with family members or agents even when we want them to have access. Someone who wants their adult child to be able to talk to doctors and get medical updates needs to sign HIPAA authorization specifically naming that child, because the general power of attorney doesn't automatically grant access to medical records, and family members trying to help manage healthcare without HIPAA authorization face doctors who legally can't share information or discuss care.

The letter of instruction provides non-legal guidance to executors and family members about funeral preferences, location of important documents, account numbers and passwords, people to notify, and other practical information that helps survivors handle immediate tasks after our death. Someone who documents their preference for cremation versus burial, what should happen with their pets, which charities they want memorial donations sent to, and where to find account statements and important papers makes the executor's job much easier and ensures their preferences get followed even for details that aren't legally binding but matter to them.

The digital asset planning addresses what happens to online accounts, digital photos, cryptocurrency, domain names, and other electronic property that didn't exist when traditional estate planning developed, and many online services have terms of service that prevent account access after death without specific authorization. Someone with $50,000 in Bitcoin stored in online wallets needs to ensure their executor or beneficiaries have the passwords and recovery information to access those assets, because cryptocurrency generally can't be recovered if access credentials are lost, turning $50,000 in assets into $0 for heirs who can't access the wallet.

The life insurance coordination with estate planning involves reviewing whether life insurance should pay to the estate or directly to beneficiaries, and whether a trust should own the policy to remove it from the taxable estate for people with estates large enough to face estate taxes. Someone with $2 million in life insurance who lives in a state with estate tax might want an irrevocable life insurance trust to own the policy so it doesn't count toward the taxable estate, potentially saving their heirs hundreds of thousands in estate taxes, while someone with a modest estate should probably just name individual beneficiaries directly and avoid the complexity of a trust.

The guardianship designation for minor children in the will specifies who should raise our children if both parents die, and this becomes urgent for parents of young children because dying without naming a guardian leaves the decision to courts who might choose family members we wouldn't have selected. Someone who wants their sister to raise their children rather than the children's other set of grandparents needs to name the sister as guardian in their will, and while this isn't absolutely binding on courts, judges typically honor the parents' stated preference unless there's strong reason not to, making it much more likely the children end up with the guardian we chose.

The testamentary trusts created in wills that don't take effect until death can protect assets for minor children or beneficiaries with special needs, providing a trustee with instructions on how to manage and distribute assets over time rather than giving large lump sums to young or vulnerable beneficiaries. Someone who dies leaving $500,000 to teenage children might establish a testamentary trust that holds the money until each child reaches 25 or 30, giving the trustee authority to distribute funds for education and basic needs but protecting the principal until the children are mature enough to handle large sums, preventing an 18-year-old from blowing through their entire inheritance on bad decisions.

The special needs trust protects assets intended for disabled beneficiaries who receive means-tested government benefits like Medicaid or SSI, allowing the trust to provide supplemental resources without disqualifying the beneficiary from essential benefits. Someone with a disabled adult child receiving Medicaid and SSI who wants to leave them $200,000 needs a properly structured special needs trust to hold those funds, because an outright inheritance would make the child ineligible for Medicaid until they spent down the $200,000, potentially leaving them without healthcare coverage, while a special needs trust can supplement their care without affecting benefit eligibility.

The estate tax exemption of $13.61 million per person in 2024 means most estates pay no federal estate tax, and only estates above this threshold face the 40% federal estate tax on amounts exceeding the exemption, though some states impose estate taxes at much lower thresholds starting at $1 million or less. Someone dying in 2024 with $15 million in assets pays federal estate tax on roughly $1.4 million at 40% rate for about $560,000 in taxes, while someone with $10 million pays no federal estate tax, and someone dying in Massachusetts or Oregon with $2 million faces state estate taxes even though they're well under the federal exemption.

The portability of estate tax exemption between spouses allows a surviving spouse to use their deceased spouse's unused exemption, effectively giving couples a combined exemption of over $27 million in 2024, but this requires filing an estate tax return after the first spouse's death even if no tax is owed to elect portability. Someone whose spouse dies with an estate of $8 million has $5.61 million of unused exemption that the survivor can add to their own $13.61 million for a total of $19.22 million, but only if they file IRS Form 706 to make the portability election within nine months of death.

The step-up in basis for inherited assets resets the cost basis to fair market value at death, eliminating capital gains on appreciation that occurred during the deceased person's lifetime, and this creates significant tax savings for beneficiaries who inherit highly appreciated assets. Someone who bought stock for $50,000 that's now worth $300,000 has $250,000 in unrealized gains, and if they sell before death they pay $37,500-50,000 in capital gains tax, but if they hold until death their heirs receive the stock with a basis of $300,000 and can sell immediately with zero capital gains tax, saving tens of thousands through the basis step-up.

The inherited IRA rules under the SECURE Act require most non-spouse beneficiaries to withdraw the entire inherited IRA within 10 years, and the distributions are taxable each year as ordinary income, creating potential bunching of income that pushes heirs into high tax brackets. Someone inheriting $600,000 Traditional IRA from a parent needs to withdraw $60,000 annually on average over 10 years, and if they're earning $80,000 from work, this adds $60,000 to their income potentially pushing them from the 22% bracket into the 24% or 32% bracket on some of the IRA distributions, costing thousands more in taxes than if the distributions could be spread over their lifetime.

The Roth conversion strategy for estate planning involves converting Traditional IRA to Roth during our lifetime to leave heirs Roth accounts rather than Traditional accounts, and while we pay the conversion taxes, our heirs receive assets that distribute tax-free even under the 10-year rule. Someone who converts $400,000 from Traditional to Roth over several years paying perhaps $80,000-100,000 in taxes leaves heirs $300,000-320,000 in Roth that generates zero taxable income during the 10-year distribution period, while leaving $400,000 in Traditional IRA creates $400,000 in taxable income for heirs over 10 years potentially costing them $80,000-120,000 in taxes depending on their tax brackets.

The community property states including California, Texas, Arizona, Nevada, Washington, Idaho, New Mexico, Louisiana, and Wisconsin have different rules for marital property where assets acquired during marriage belong equally to both spouses regardless of whose name they're in, and this affects how assets transfer at death and what gets basis step-up. Someone dying in California with a house bought during marriage gets full basis step-up on the entire house even if only their half of the community property interest passes through their estate, while someone in a common-law property state only gets step-up on their individual share, creating different tax outcomes from the same scenario based solely on which state they live in.

The annual gift tax exclusion of $18,000 per person in 2024 allows us to give this amount to unlimited recipients each year without filing gift tax returns or using any of our lifetime estate tax exemption, and couples can combine their exclusions to give $36,000 per recipient annually. Someone with three adult children and six grandchildren can give $162,000 per year total across the nine recipients without any gift tax implications, and a married couple can give $324,000 annually to the same nine people, transferring substantial wealth out of their taxable estate while maintaining the annual exclusion.

The 529 education account superfunding allows contributing five years of annual exclusions upfront as a lump sum, letting grandparents or parents contribute $90,000 per beneficiary or $180,000 as a couple, immediately transferring substantial assets for education while removing them from the taxable estate. Someone with $200,000 they want to dedicate to a grandchild's education can contribute $180,000 to a 529 plan in a single year by using the five-year acceleration, removing this amount from their estate immediately while maintaining control over the account as owner, though they can't make additional annual exclusion gifts to that grandchild for the next five years.

The review and update of estate documents every 3-5 years or after major life events like marriage, divorce, birth, death, or significant wealth changes ensures that plans remain current and aligned with intentions, and documents drafted 20 years ago might not reflect current laws, family circumstances, or our wishes. Someone whose will was drafted before they had grandchildren or before a child's divorce might want to update to include grandchildren as beneficiaries or to protect assets from a child's ex-spouse through trust provisions, and reviewing documents regularly prevents discovering too late that plans are outdated and don't accomplish what we now want.

Estate planning assumes there will be an estate. Long-term care is the single largest threat to that assumption. Nursing home costs can consume decades of careful saving in a few years, and most retirement plans treat this risk as something that happens to other people. The statistics suggest otherwise.

The Expense Most People Skip

The statistics on long-term care needs show that roughly 70% of people over 65 will need some form of long-term care during their lifetime, whether home health assistance, assisted living, or nursing home care, and while the percentage is high, the duration and intensity vary enormously from a few months of home care after surgery to years in a nursing home with advanced dementia. Someone planning for retirement needs to account for the possibility of spending $50,000-100,000 annually on care for several years, and the uncertainty about whether we'll be in the 30% who never need care or the 70% who do creates difficult planning decisions about insurance, asset protection, and savings adequacy.

Nursing home costs average $105,000 per year nationally in 2024 for a private room, though costs vary from $75,000 in some areas to $150,000 or more in expensive markets, and these costs increase roughly 4-5% annually, substantially faster than general inflation. Someone who enters a nursing home at 82 and lives there for three years faces total costs of $315,000-450,000 depending on location and whether costs increase during their stay, and this represents a catastrophic expense that depletes retirement savings built over decades in just a few years unless we have long-term care insurance or substantial assets to self-insure.

Assisted living costs run lower at $54,000-72,000 annually on average, providing housing, meals, and basic assistance with activities of daily living for people who need help but not the intensive nursing care that nursing homes provide. Someone who can't live independently but doesn't need skilled nursing might spend 5-7 years in assisted living costing $270,000-500,000 total before either recovering enough to return home or declining enough to require nursing home placement, and while assisted living costs less per year than nursing homes, the longer average stays can create similar or higher total costs.

Home health care costs vary by intensity and location, ranging from $25-35 per hour for home health aides to $50-100 per hour for skilled nursing visits, and someone who needs daily assistance might spend $30,000-70,000 annually on home care depending on how many hours per day they require help. The advantage of home care is that it's scalable to actual needs, starting with a few hours per week for light assistance and increasing to round-the-clock care if needed, while institutional care comes in larger chunks where we pay full nursing home rates regardless of whether we need that much care.

Activities of daily living including bathing, dressing, eating, toileting, transferring from bed to chair, and continence determine eligibility for insurance benefits and Medicaid coverage, and someone who can't independently perform two or three of these ADLs typically qualifies for long-term care benefits. The loss of ADL independence often comes gradually, starting with difficulty bathing or dressing and progressing over months or years to needing help with eating and toileting, and the progressive nature means we might need increasingly intensive care over time rather than suddenly requiring full nursing home care.

Long-term care insurance policies pay benefits when we meet certain criteria, typically inability to perform two ADLs independently or cognitive impairment requiring supervision, and the benefits cover nursing home care, assisted living, and home care up to the policy's daily or monthly maximum. Someone with a policy paying $200 per day for up to four years has $292,000 in total coverage that can be used for nursing home care at $290 per day or assisted living at $150 per day or home care at whatever hourly rate they need, though many policies have different coverage levels or restrictions for different care settings.

The cost of long-term care insurance varies dramatically by age at purchase, with someone buying at 55 paying perhaps $2,500-3,500 annually for reasonable coverage while someone waiting until 65 pays $4,000-6,000 annually for the same coverage, and premiums can increase over time as insurance companies raise rates on entire classes of policies. Someone who buys coverage at 55 and pays $3,000 annually for 30 years until age 85 spends $90,000 in premiums, and if they then need care for three years, the policy might pay out $200,000-250,000 in benefits, providing positive return on the premium investment if care is needed but creating $90,000 in sunk costs if they never need care.

The premium increases on older long-term care insurance policies have been substantial because insurance companies underpriced policies in the 1990s and 2000s, and policyholders who thought they had stable premiums have seen increases of 50-100% or more, turning what seemed like affordable coverage into a burden. Someone who bought a policy for $2,000 annually in 2000 might now be paying $4,000-5,000 annually after multiple rate increases, and they face the difficult choice of continuing to pay increased premiums to maintain coverage they've paid into for decades or dropping the policy and losing all the premiums already paid.

The hybrid life insurance with long-term care riders combines life insurance death benefit with long-term care coverage, allowing us to access the death benefit for care if needed while preserving a smaller death benefit for heirs if we don't use the care benefits. Someone who buys a $300,000 hybrid policy might be able to access up to $250,000 for long-term care over their lifetime, and if they use $100,000 for care, the remaining $200,000 goes to beneficiaries at death, avoiding the use-it-or-lose-it problem of traditional long-term care insurance where all premiums are lost if we never need care.

The single premium option for hybrid policies involves paying a large upfront amount of $75,000-150,000 to fund the policy permanently with no ongoing premiums, and this appeals to people who have assets they want to earmark for long-term care while maintaining access through the life insurance death benefit. Someone who pays $100,000 for a hybrid policy with $300,000 life insurance death benefit and $250,000 long-term care pool has $100,000 less in liquid assets but knows that either they'll get the long-term care coverage if needed or their heirs will get $300,000 at death, avoiding the scenario where $100,000 in traditional long-term care insurance premiums buys nothing if care is never needed.

Medicaid covers long-term care for people who meet income and asset limits, effectively serving as the long-term care insurance of last resort for people who spend down their assets paying for care privately until they're poor enough to qualify for government coverage. The income limits are roughly $2,900 per month in 2024 though this varies by state, and the asset limits are typically $2,000 for individuals or $3,000 for couples, meaning someone with $400,000 in savings must spend down to $2,000 before qualifying for Medicaid nursing home coverage.

The spend-down process for Medicaid requires paying privately for care until assets fall below the threshold, and someone entering a nursing home with $300,000 in assets paying $105,000 annually depletes their assets in about three years and then qualifies for Medicaid coverage. The community spouse resource allowance protects some assets for the spouse still living at home, letting them keep roughly $154,000 in 2024 plus the house and one vehicle, while the nursing home spouse must spend down to $2,000, creating scenarios where couples see most of their savings consumed by one spouse's care while the other spouse maintains minimal resources for their own future needs.

The five-year lookback for Medicaid scrutinizes all asset transfers and gifts made in the five years before applying for benefits, and any transfers for less than fair value create periods of Medicaid ineligibility based on the amount transferred. Someone who gives $100,000 to their children two years before entering a nursing home and then applies for Medicaid faces a penalty period where Medicaid won't pay, calculated by dividing the transfer amount by the average monthly cost of nursing home care in their state, potentially creating 10-15 months of ineligibility where they must pay privately or the family must pay.

The irrevocable Medicaid trust protects assets from spend-down requirements if established at least five years before needing care, and assets transferred to the trust count for the five-year lookback but then become protected once the lookback period expires. Someone who transfers $400,000 to an irrevocable Medicaid trust at age 68 gives up control of those assets but potentially protects them from nursing home spend-down requirements if they need care after age 73, preserving the $400,000 for children or the community spouse, though the trade-off is losing access to those assets during the years before needing care when they might want to use the money for travel or other retirement goals.

The penalty for Medicaid planning is that we're transferring assets to protect them from care costs rather than using them for our own care, and someone who gives away $300,000 to protect it from nursing home costs but then gets inadequate care on Medicaid might regret not keeping the money to pay for private care with better facilities and more options. The nursing homes that accept Medicaid often provide lower quality care than private-pay facilities, and someone who protected assets through Medicaid planning might spend years in a substandard facility rather than using their own money for quality private care.

The ethical question around Medicaid planning involves whether middle-class people should structure their finances to qualify for need-based government benefits by artificially impoverishing themselves through asset transfers, and while this is legal, it raises questions about using limited government resources intended for people without means. Someone with $500,000 who could afford to pay for their own care for several years but instead transfers assets to qualify for Medicaid immediately is technically following the rules but arguably taking benefits from people who truly have no other options.

Self-insuring through adequate savings means maintaining portfolio balances large enough to cover potential long-term care costs without insurance, accepting the risk that we might spend $300,000-500,000 on care over several years but knowing we have the assets to cover it. Someone with $2 million in retirement assets can probably self-insure against long-term care costs because even spending $400,000 on care leaves $1.6 million for the surviving spouse or heirs, while someone with $500,000 faces potential portfolio depletion if they need extensive care, making insurance or Medicaid planning more important.

The decision between insurance and self-insurance depends on our risk tolerance, asset level, family health history, and how much we value control over care versus protecting assets for heirs. Someone with $800,000 in assets and strong family history of dementia might buy long-term care insurance to protect their spouse and assets from catastrophic care costs, while someone with $2 million and no family history of needing care might skip insurance and self-insure, accepting that care might cost $300,000-500,000 but knowing they have adequate assets to cover it without insurance premiums.

The elimination period in long-term care insurance policies is the waiting period before benefits begin, typically 30, 60, or 90 days during which we pay for care out of pocket before insurance starts paying. Someone with a 90-day elimination period entering a nursing home at $290 per day pays roughly $26,000 out of pocket before insurance benefits begin, and shorter elimination periods cost more in premiums but reduce out-of-pocket costs, creating trade-offs between premium costs and early care costs.

The inflation protection riders increase policy benefits by 3-5% annually or compound the daily benefit to account for rising care costs, and while these riders significantly increase premiums, care costs decades from now will be much higher than current costs. Someone buying a policy at 55 with $200 daily benefit and 3% compound inflation has that benefit grow to $400 per day by age 80, keeping pace roughly with actual care cost increases, while someone without inflation protection might find their $200 daily benefit covers only half the actual cost of care when they need it 25 years later.

The tax deductibility of long-term care insurance premiums as medical expenses provides some offset to premium costs for people who itemize deductions and have total medical expenses exceeding 7.5% of AGI, though most people can't deduct the premiums because they don't itemize or their medical expenses don't exceed the threshold. Someone with $80,000 in AGI needs more than $6,000 in medical expenses to get any deduction, and if their long-term care insurance premium is $4,000 annually plus $3,000 in other medical expenses, they can deduct $1,000, saving perhaps $220-320 in taxes depending on their bracket.

The partnership programs in many states allow people who buy qualified long-term care insurance policies to protect additional assets beyond the normal Medicaid limits by the amount the insurance pays out, creating incentives to buy coverage while providing some asset protection. Someone who buys a partnership policy and receives $150,000 in benefits from the insurance can then qualify for Medicaid while keeping $152,000 in assets instead of the normal $2,000 limit, protecting assets equal to what the insurance paid out, and while this doesn't preserve the entire estate, it provides better asset protection than going straight to Medicaid spend-down.

Veterans benefits through the VA Aid and Attendance program can provide up to $2,300 per month for wartime veterans or their surviving spouses who need help with activities of daily living, and while this doesn't cover full nursing home costs, it can substantially offset assisted living or home care expenses. Someone who served during a war period and now needs care assistance might qualify for this benefit that provides $27,600 annually toward care costs, and combined with other income, this might cover assisted living completely or reduce out-of-pocket costs for home care.

The family caregiving alternative to paid care involves adult children or other relatives providing care at home, and while this saves money on paid care, it creates other costs including lost wages for the caregiver, emotional and physical stress, and potential family conflict. Someone whose adult child quits their job to provide full-time care saves $50,000-70,000 annually in paid care costs but the child loses $40,000-60,000 in wages plus career advancement, and the arrangement might work initially but break down after a year or two when the caregiver burns out from the physical and emotional demands.

The respite care provides temporary relief for family caregivers through paid help for a few hours per week or short-term nursing home stays for a week or two, allowing caregivers to rest, travel, or handle their own obligations without completely abandoning the care arrangement. Someone providing full-time care for a spouse with dementia might use respite care for two weeks annually to take a vacation, maintaining their own mental health and ability to continue caregiving long-term, and many long-term care insurance policies cover respite care as part of their benefits.

The continuing care retirement communities combine independent living, assisted living, and nursing home care in one campus, allowing residents to age in place by moving to higher levels of care as needed while staying in the same community. Someone who moves to a CCRC at 70 while healthy might live independently for 10-15 years, then move to assisted living for 3-5 years, then finish life in the nursing home wing, and the buy-in fees of $200,000-500,000 plus monthly fees of $3,000-6,000 cover housing and eventual care needs, providing certainty about care access but requiring large upfront payments.

The life care contracts at CCRCs include future healthcare and long-term care in the monthly fee regardless of how much care is needed, while fee-for-service contracts charge market rates for higher levels of care when needed, and the choice depends on health expectations and risk tolerance. Someone who expects to need extensive care might prefer a life care contract that locks in all-inclusive pricing even if monthly fees are $1,000-2,000 higher, while someone who expects to stay healthy might choose fee-for-service and pay lower fees while healthy, accepting the risk of higher costs if they eventually need care.

The overall strategy for long-term care planning involves assessing our asset level and risk tolerance to decide between insurance, self-insurance, or Medicaid planning, considering hybrid insurance products that preserve some value if care isn't needed, understanding the five-year lookback rules if Medicaid planning might be necessary, having honest family discussions about care preferences and financial resources, and recognizing that the uncertainty around whether we'll need care and how much creates legitimate disagreement about the right approach rather than a single correct answer.

Long-term care intersects with the legal and financial realities of marriage in ways that can be devastating without planning and manageable with it. But marriage itself — and divorce, and remarriage — changes retirement math in ways that go well beyond long-term care. The people we're married to, and when, affect Social Security, taxes, healthcare, and asset protection in ways that deserve their own treatment.

When Life Changes the Numbers

Marriage creates automatic financial entanglements including joint liability for debts incurred during marriage in community property states, rights to inherit from each other even without a will, Social Security spousal and survivor benefits based on the higher earner's record, and combined income for tax purposes that can push couples into higher brackets or reduce eligibility for income-tested benefits. Someone who marries at 55 with $800,000 in retirement accounts and a house worth $400,000 suddenly faces estate planning questions about whether these assets should go to their new spouse or to children from a previous marriage, tax planning around combined income that might trigger IRMAA or reduce ACA subsidies, and Social Security strategy decisions that now involve coordinating two people's claiming ages.

The tax filing status changes from single to married filing jointly or married filing separately, and while joint filing usually provides lower taxes through higher standard deductions and wider tax brackets, situations exist where married filing separately makes sense to protect one spouse from the other's tax liabilities or to optimize income-tested benefits. A couple where one spouse owes back taxes or has complex business income with potential audit issues might file separately to insulate the other spouse from tax problems, accepting higher overall tax rates in exchange for separation of liability, while a couple where both have high incomes and are paying IRMAA might file separately if it reduces total Medicare premiums despite increasing income taxes.

The marriage penalty in tax brackets affects high-earning couples where combining incomes pushes them into higher brackets than they'd face as singles, and two people each earning $200,000 who marry see their combined $400,000 taxed partly in the 35% bracket as a married couple versus having significant amounts in the 32% bracket as singles. The penalty costs roughly $7,000-10,000 annually for couples with similar high incomes, making marriage financially costly from a pure tax perspective, though the benefits of joint tax filing for most couples outweigh this penalty and the marriage decision obviously involves factors beyond tax optimization.

The Social Security spousal benefit allows a lower-earning spouse to receive up to 50% of the higher earner's full retirement age benefit instead of their own benefit if that provides more income, and this requires being married for at least one year before the lower earner applies for spousal benefits. Someone who marries at 64 and wants to claim spousal benefits at 66 needs to wait until 65 to satisfy the one-year marriage requirement, and the spousal benefit maxes out at 50% of the higher earner's PIA when both spouses claim at full retirement age, dropping to 32-35% if claimed at 62.

The Social Security survivor benefit provides the surviving spouse the higher of the two spouses' benefits when one dies, and this requires being married for at least nine months before death except for accidental death where the requirement is waived. Someone whose spouse dies at 68 after two years of marriage qualifies for survivor benefits, but someone whose spouse dies at 67 after eight months of marriage doesn't qualify because the nine-month requirement wasn't met, creating situations where the duration of marriage by just a few weeks determines whether the survivor receives benefits or not.

The Medicare premium for the surviving spouse continues at whatever rate they were paying, including IRMAA surcharges based on their own income from two years prior, and when household income drops from two Social Security checks plus portfolio withdrawals to one Social Security check and smaller withdrawals, the surviving spouse might find themselves in lower IRMAA brackets. Someone whose household income was $180,000 combined paying no IRMAA might see the survivor's income drop to $80,000, eliminating IRMAA two years after the income change when the lookback period catches up, potentially saving $2,000-3,000 annually in Medicare premiums.

Divorce after 10 years of marriage preserves the right to claim divorced spouse benefits on the ex's Social Security record, receiving up to 50% of the ex's full retirement age benefit without affecting what the ex receives or even requiring the ex to know about the claim. Someone divorced after

11 years can claim divorced spouse benefits at their full retirement age, or reduced benefits as early as 62, as long as they remain unmarried, and this provides retirement income based on the ex's higher earnings even though the marriage ended decades ago. Someone divorced after nine years and 11 months gets nothing from the ex's Social Security despite nearly a decade of marriage, making the 10-year threshold absolute and occasionally motivating couples to delay divorce by a few weeks to cross the threshold.

The division of retirement accounts in divorce through Qualified Domestic Relations Orders allows splitting 401k and pension accounts without triggering early withdrawal penalties or immediate taxes, and the receiving spouse can roll their portion into their own IRA and treat it as their own retirement asset. Someone divorcing at 55 with $600,000 in 401k who splits it 50-50 with their spouse sees each person get $300,000, and the spouse receiving the QDRO transfer can roll the $300,000 to IRA immediately with no taxes or penalties, maintaining the tax-deferred status until they eventually withdraw the money in retirement.

The immediate access exception under QDRO rules allows the receiving spouse to withdraw the transferred amount immediately if they choose without the 10% early withdrawal penalty even if under 59.5, though they still pay income tax on the amount withdrawn. Someone receiving $200,000 through QDRO at age 48 can withdraw $50,000 immediately to fund the divorce transition, pay income tax on the $50,000 at their ordinary income rate, but avoid the $5,000 early withdrawal penalty that would normally apply, and this one-time ability to access retirement money penalty-free can provide needed liquidity during divorce when legal fees and housing transitions create cash demands.

The alimony tax treatment changed under the Tax Cuts and Jobs Act where alimony payments for divorces finalized after 2018 are neither deductible for the payer nor taxable for the recipient, while divorces finalized before 2019 still follow the old rules where alimony is deductible for the payer and taxable to the recipient. Someone paying $30,000 annually in alimony under a 2017 divorce agreement deducts it from taxable income, saving $7,000-11,000 in federal taxes depending on their bracket, while someone paying the same amount under a 2020 divorce gets no deduction and the recipient pays no tax on the income.

The property division in divorce varies by state between community property states where assets acquired during marriage split 50-50 and equitable distribution states where courts divide assets based on various factors including income, earning potential, length of marriage, and contribution to asset acquisition. Someone divorcing in California after 20 years sees assets accumulated during those 20 years split equally regardless of whose name they're in or who earned the money, while someone divorcing in New York might see an unequal division where the higher earner keeps 60-70% of marital assets based on their greater income and future earning capacity.

The separate property versus marital property distinction determines which assets get divided in divorce, with separate property including assets owned before marriage, inheritances received during marriage, and gifts received from third parties remaining with the original owner, while marital property gets divided. Someone who entered marriage with $300,000 in retirement accounts and those accounts grew to $500,000 during a 10-year marriage might keep the original $300,000 as separate property while the $200,000 growth gets split as marital property, though commingling separate and marital funds in the same account can make the entire account marital property if not properly tracked.

The health insurance continuation through COBRA after divorce allows the spouse who was covered under the working spouse's employer plan to continue coverage for up to 36 months by paying the full premium plus 2% administrative fee, providing a bridge to either finding their own employer coverage or reaching Medicare age. Someone divorcing at 63 who was on their spouse's employer health insurance can maintain that coverage through COBRA until 66 when Medicare becomes available, paying perhaps $800-1,000 monthly for family coverage that only covers them individually after divorce, though this might be cheaper than ACA marketplace coverage for someone in their early 60s.

The prenuptial agreements before marriage or postnuptial agreements during marriage can specify how assets will be divided if the marriage ends, protecting assets accumulated before marriage or inherited during marriage and potentially avoiding lengthy divorce litigation. Someone entering a second marriage at 60 with $1 million in assets and adult children from the first marriage might use a prenup stating that the $1 million remains separate property going to their children at death while assets accumulated during the second marriage get split with the new spouse, providing clarity and protecting the children's inheritance while still sharing new marital assets with the spouse.

The retirement age coordination between spouses affects claiming strategy and withdrawal planning, and couples where both spouses are similar ages might retire together while couples with significant age gaps face decisions about whether the younger spouse keeps working while the older spouse retires. Someone who is 67 married to someone who is 58 might retire and claim Social Security while the younger spouse continues working for nine more years, living on one Social Security check plus portfolio withdrawals until both are retired, or they might delay their own retirement to 70 to let their benefit grow while enjoying the younger spouse's income and health insurance.

Remarriage after divorce or death of spouse creates new Social Security considerations because remarrying before age 60 eliminates eligibility for divorced spouse or survivor benefits from the previous marriage, while remarrying at 60 or later preserves those benefits. Someone widowed at 58 who remarries at 59 loses the right to survivor benefits from their deceased spouse, while waiting until 60 to remarry preserves survivor benefits that might be larger than their own benefit or a spousal benefit from the new spouse, potentially providing thousands more in annual income over retirement.

The estate planning complications in second marriages involve balancing provision for the new spouse against protecting inheritances for children from the first marriage, and common strategies include life insurance trusts, Qualified Terminable Interest Property trusts, or specific bequests of separate property assets. Someone with $800,000 in assets and children from a first marriage who remarries at 65 might structure their estate plan to provide the new spouse a life estate in the house and income from half the portfolio, with the principal going to the children at the second spouse's death, ensuring the spouse isn't left destitute while still protecting the children's eventual inheritance.

The family dynamics in blended families create tensions around money, inheritances, and support that couples in first marriages don't typically face, and someone whose adult children expect to inherit their assets might resent seeing those assets used to support a new spouse or step-siblings. The conversations about estate planning, retirement spending, and financial support need to happen early in second marriages to prevent conflict later when health issues or death force decisions about asset distribution and care provision, and couples who avoid these discussions often leave surviving family members fighting over estates or feeling betrayed by dispositions they didn't expect.

The income taxation of married couples requires combining all income sources from both spouses and filing jointly or separately, and the combination can push couples into higher brackets or create IRMAA surcharges where neither individual alone would face these higher rates. Someone with $80,000 in retirement income married to someone with $70,000 in retirement income files jointly showing $150,000 combined income that triggers the first IRMAA tier, adding $2,000-3,000 annually to Medicare premiums for each spouse that they wouldn't pay if they remained single, effectively creating a marriage penalty specifically for Medicare costs.

The ACA subsidy cliff that exists when enhanced subsidies expire makes marriage financially devastating for some early retirees who lose subsidies entirely when combining income pushes them above the 400% FPL threshold, and two people each receiving $10,000 annually in ACA subsidies as singles might lose both subsidies worth $20,000 total if marrying combines their MAGI above the threshold. The perverse incentive to delay marriage or cohabitate without marrying to preserve healthcare subsidies creates situations where people make major life decisions based on arbitrary income thresholds rather than relationship preferences, and couples might choose to delay marriage from 60 to 65 specifically to preserve ACA subsidies worth tens of thousands of dollars.

The long-term care considerations in late-life marriages involve questions about whether new spouses will provide care for each other or whether care responsibilities fall to adult children from previous marriages, and the financial implications of one spouse's long-term care depleting shared assets meant to support the other spouse's retirement. Someone who marries at 70 and then needs nursing home care at 78 might see their half of marital assets plus some of the new spouse's assets consumed by care costs, leaving the healthy spouse with reduced resources, and prenuptial agreements or asset segregation strategies can protect against this but require difficult conversations about care expectations and financial separation.

The widow or widower's challenge in dating and potentially remarrying involves balancing the loneliness and desire for companionship against the financial and emotional complexities of late-life marriage, and someone who lost a spouse after 40 years of marriage might find dating in their 70s completely different from when they were young. The financial questions about combining assets, protecting inheritances, managing income and taxes, and planning for eventual care needs combine with emotional questions about honoring the first spouse's memory, integrating new partners into existing family structures, and managing adult children's reactions to create situations where companionship without marriage becomes appealing despite the lack of legal protections and benefits.

The legal protections of marriage including next-of-kin status for medical decisions, automatic inheritance rights, and Social Security benefits create value beyond just emotional partnership, and someone who cohabitates without marrying needs healthcare powers of attorney, updated wills naming the partner, and potentially life insurance to replace benefits that marriage would provide automatically. The decision between marriage and cohabitation for older adults involves weighing these legal protections and benefits against the financial complications of combining estates, dealing with adult children's objections, and potentially facing IRMAA or ACA subsidy penalties from combined income.

All of the separate pieces — the accounts, the Social Security strategy, the healthcare planning, the withdrawal sequencing, the location choices, the estate plan — only produce their full value when they work together. The integration is where most people lose ground, making individually reasonable decisions that don't coordinate well and leaving tens of thousands on the table as a result.

How the Pieces Connect

The complete retirement plan integrates everything from savings rates during working years through withdrawal strategies in retirement, and someone who understands each component but fails to coordinate them into a coherent whole might make individually reasonable decisions that don't work well together, like maximizing Traditional 401k contributions during high earning years without considering the RMD tax bomb this creates in retirement, or claiming Social Security at 62 without accounting for the impact on spousal survivor benefits decades later. The integration requires thinking across 40-50 year timelines from age 30 to 80 and considering how decisions in one decade affect outcomes in another decade, creating complexity that's difficult to manage but essential for optimizing lifetime financial security.

Someone earning $80,000 at age 35 with $50,000 saved needs to calculate how much to contribute to 401k versus Roth IRA versus taxable accounts, whether to pursue aggressive Roth conversions in low-income years, when to claim Social Security to maximize lifetime benefits considering spousal coordination, how to sequence withdrawals from different account types to minimize taxes and preserve subsidies, whether to buy long-term care insurance or self-insure, and when to retire based on portfolio size and spending needs. Each decision affects the others, and the optimal choice for 401k contributions depends on expected retirement tax rates which depend on withdrawal sequencing which depends on Social Security claiming age which depends on health and longevity expectations.

The starting point involves calculating the real retirement spending number based on current expenses adjusted for known changes like paying off mortgages, eliminating commute and work costs, adding healthcare expenses, and accounting for inflation over potentially 30-40 years of retirement. Someone currently spending $65,000 annually might project retirement spending of $55,000 after eliminating $7,000 in commute and work expenses and $3,000 in mortgage payments that will finish before retirement, but then adding $12,000 in healthcare costs before Medicare and

$8,000 after Medicare brings the number back to $55,000-60,000 depending on age, and inflating this at 3% annually means spending grows from $55,000 at 65 to $75,000 at 75 to $100,000 at 85.

The portfolio target emerges from the spending calculation combined with Social Security estimates and desired withdrawal rate, and someone needing $60,000 annually who expects $28,000 in Social Security requires $32,000 from portfolio, which at 4% withdrawal rate means $800,000 saved by retirement. If they plan to retire at 62 instead of 67, the Social Security drops to $20,000 and required portfolio increases to $1,000,000, and if they want to maintain $60,000 spending until 90 rather than just to life expectancy of 85, the required portfolio might increase another $100,000-150,000 to provide cushion against portfolio depletion, bringing the total target to $1,100,000-1,150,000 for retirement at 62.

The savings rate to hit the target depends on current age, years until retirement, current savings, and expected returns, and someone who is 40 with $150,000 saved who needs $1,000,000 by 65 must save roughly $16,000 annually at 7% returns, while waiting until 45 to start saving that same $16,000 annually only accumulates $650,000, creating a $350,000 shortfall that requires either working until 72, reducing retirement spending by $14,000 annually, moving to a cheaper location, or accepting higher portfolio failure risk. The compounding impact of starting earlier versus later means that someone who saves $10,000 annually from 30-40 and then stops accumulates more by 65 than someone who saves $10,000 annually from 50-65, demonstrating that time in the market matters more than timing the market or contribution amounts.

The Roth versus Traditional choice during accumulation depends on current marginal tax rate versus expected retirement marginal rate, and someone in the 24% bracket now who expects to be in the 12% bracket in retirement should use Traditional contributions to get the deduction at 24% and pay tax later at 12%, while someone in the 12% bracket now who expects higher rates in retirement from large RMDs should use Roth contributions to pay tax now at low rates. The complication is that we don't know future tax rates or our retirement income with certainty, which argues for diversification between Roth and Traditional to hedge against different scenarios, and someone who puts 60-70% in Traditional and 30-40% in Roth during working years creates flexibility in retirement to manage taxable income through selective withdrawals.

The early retirement strategy requires building substantial taxable account balances or Roth conversion ladders to fund the years between leaving work and accessing retirement accounts at 59.5, and someone retiring at 55 needs either $200,000-300,000 in taxable accounts to fund 4.5 years of spending at $45,000-65,000 annually, or needs to start Roth conversions at 50 to create a pipeline of accessible money through the five-year conversion aging process. The alternative is using 72(t) substantially equal periodic payments to access IRA money before 59.5, but this locks us into fixed withdrawals for at least five years and creates penalties if we modify the arrangement, making it less flexible than having taxable or Roth money available.

The ACA subsidy optimization from 60-65 for early retirees involves building Roth balances during working years that can be withdrawn without creating MAGI during subsidy years, and someone who does $30,000 annual Roth conversions from 50-59 creates $300,000 in Roth that can fund living expenses from 60-65 while keeping MAGI at $20,000-30,000 to maximize subsidies worth $8,000-12,000 annually. The $40,000-50,000 paid in conversion taxes from 50-59 gets repaid through $40,000-60,000 in ACA subsidies from 60-65, and the remaining Roth balance provides tax-free income for the rest of retirement, making the conversion strategy both tax-efficient and subsidy-optimizing.

The Social Security claiming coordination for married couples typically involves the higher earner delaying to 70 to maximize survivor benefits while the lower earner claims somewhere between 62 and full retirement age depending on cash flow needs and their own benefit size relative to spousal benefits. A couple where one spouse has PIA of $2,800 and the other has PIA of $1,200 sees optimal outcomes when the $2,800 earner delays to 70 receiving $3,472 and the $1,200 earner claims at 64 receiving roughly $1,000, providing combined income of $4,472 while both are alive and

$3,472 to the survivor, versus claiming both at 62 providing $3,458 combined and only $1,946 to the survivor.

The Medicare planning involves timing Roth conversions to avoid IRMAA during the two-year lookback period after enrolling at 65, which means someone retiring at 60 can do aggressive conversions from 60-62 showing high MAGI that won't affect Medicare until age 64-66 when they can file life-changing event appeals to remove IRMAA based on current retirement income. The alternative is doing conversions from 66-72 after the initial Medicare enrollment period, accepting IRMAA during conversion years but avoiding it during the vulnerable initial period when we're learning the Medicare system and might not know about appeals, and the choice depends on total conversion amounts and whether we're comfortable managing the appeal process.

The withdrawal sequencing in retirement coordinates taxable account drawdowns during ACA years, partial Roth conversions before RMDs begin, strategic capital gains harvesting at 0% rates, and Social Security claiming timing to minimize lifetime taxes while maintaining adequate cash flow. Someone retiring at 60 might spend taxable account principal plus Roth contributions from 60-65 keeping MAGI at $25,000, start Traditional IRA withdrawals at 65 taking $35,000 annually to fill the 12% bracket and do small Roth conversions, claim Social Security at 67-70 depending on health and spousal situation, and then at 73 when RMDs begin, adjust withdrawal strategy to satisfy RMDs while supplementing from Roth as needed to avoid bracket creep.

The geographic arbitrage decision involves calculating total costs in current location versus potential lower-cost locations, accounting for housing, taxes, healthcare, and quality of life factors, and someone paying $36,000 annually in housing plus $8,000 in state and property taxes in California versus $18,000 housing plus $3,000 taxes in North Carolina saves $23,000 annually, which at 4% withdrawal rate reduces required portfolio by $575,000. The $575,000 difference might mean retiring at 60 instead of 67, or retiring with comfortable margin instead of barely adequate resources, making location choice potentially the highest-impact single decision for retirement timing and security.

The part-time work integration into the plan provides sequence of returns risk protection during the vulnerable first 5-10 years of retirement, and someone earning $20,000 annually from part-time work from 62-70 reduces portfolio withdrawals by $160,000 over those eight years, letting the portfolio grow from what might have been $800,000 to perhaps $950,000 by age 70 when they stop working. The larger portfolio plus eight more years of returns plus delayed Social Security creating higher benefits all combine to improve portfolio survival rates from perhaps 85% to 95%, turning a marginal plan into a solid plan through the flexibility to work part-time.

The long-term care planning coordinates with estate planning and asset protection, and someone with $1,200,000 in retirement assets who wants to leave $400,000 to children might buy long-term care insurance to protect that inheritance from being consumed by care costs, or might self-insure accepting that care costs could reduce the inheritance while preserving flexibility to use assets for their own quality care. The choice depends on the importance of leaving an inheritance versus maintaining full control of assets, and someone without heirs or who prioritizes their own care quality over leaving bequests might skip insurance and plan to spend everything on their own care if needed.

The estate planning integration ensures beneficiary designations align with will provisions, that retirement account beneficiaries will handle the tax consequences of inherited Traditional IRAs appropriately, that estate size stays under thresholds that trigger state estate taxes in states like Massachusetts or Oregon, and that asset titling either facilitates probate avoidance through joint ownership and beneficiaries or uses trusts when privacy and control matter. Someone with $900,000 in retirement accounts and $300,000 in other assets in Oregon faces potential state estate tax at the $1 million threshold, and they might do Roth conversions to pay taxes during lifetime reducing their taxable estate, or make annual gifts to children to transfer assets before death, or purchase life insurance owned by an irrevocable trust to provide heirs with liquid assets to pay estate taxes.

The failure mode planning involves identifying what could go wrong and having contingencies, including forced early retirement from job loss or health problems before we've saved enough, portfolio crashes early in retirement creating sequence risk, higher than expected healthcare costs from chronic illness, divorce depleting assets and eliminating spousal benefits, death of spouse creating survivor income gap, and long-term care costs consuming the portfolio. Someone whose plan assumes working until 65 should consider what happens if they're forced out at 60, whether they could reduce spending, whether part-time work is feasible, whether they could move to a cheaper location, and what the portfolio success rate looks like with five fewer years of contributions and five more years of withdrawals.

The flexibility and adaptability matter more than perfectly optimizing any single decision, and someone who builds in margin through extra savings, lower spending, willingness to work part-time, openness to geographic moves, and diversification of account types can adapt to changed circumstances much more easily than someone who optimizes for a single scenario with no backup options. The plan that works if everything goes perfectly but fails if anything goes wrong is worse than the plan that works adequately across many scenarios even if it's not perfect in any single one, and retirement planning should prioritize robustness over optimization given the 30-40 year timeline where many things will inevitably not go according to plan.

The monitoring and adjustment process involves reviewing the plan annually or when major life changes occur, checking whether we're on track to hit savings targets, whether spending assumptions still make sense, whether withdrawal rates need adjustment based on portfolio performance, whether Social Security claiming strategy should change based on health updates, and whether market conditions or tax law changes affect the optimal approach. Someone at 50 who projected needing \$1,000,000 by 65 and has \$400,000 saved is on track if they've been saving 15 years and need 15 more, but if markets have been weak and they only have \$350,000 despite adequate contributions, they need to adjust by increasing savings rate, planning to work longer, reducing spending expectations, or accepting higher risk.

The acceptance that perfect execution is impossible and that we'll make mistakes, experience bad luck, and face unexpected challenges helps maintain perspective and prevents paralysis from trying to optimize everything perfectly. Someone who spends months agonizing over whether to claim Social Security at 68 or 69 when the difference is perhaps $1,500 in annual benefits might be wasting time better spent on bigger decisions like whether to retire at 62 or 65 where the difference is $150,000-200,000 in required savings, and the good-enough approach that makes reasonable decisions on major factors and doesn't obsess over minor optimization often produces better outcomes than the perfectionist approach that gets paralyzed and makes no decisions.

The overall integrated strategy combines aggressive saving during working years with at least 15% of income going to retirement accounts, diversification between Roth and Traditional contributions to provide flexibility in retirement, building taxable account balances if planning early retirement, timing Roth conversions to avoid IRMAA around Medicare enrollment, coordinating Social Security claiming between spouses to maximize survivor benefits, sequencing withdrawals to minimize taxes and preserve subsidies when applicable, considering geographic arbitrage to reduce required savings by $300,000-600,000, using part-time work to bridge early retirement years and reduce sequence risk, and maintaining enough margin in the plan that unexpected health problems, market crashes, or forced early retirement don't create financial crisis.

The person who successfully integrates all these elements might retire at 62 with $900,000 saved and spend the next 30 years living comfortably on combined Social Security and portfolio withdrawals, helping their children financially when needed, traveling and pursuing hobbies, and eventually leaving $200,000-300,000 to heirs after covering all their own expenses including healthcare and potential long-term care. The person who saves the same amount but doesn't integrate the components well might run out of money at 80 from poor withdrawal sequencing creating unnecessarily high taxes, ill-timed Social Security claiming reducing survivor benefits, and lack of geographic flexibility preventing cost reduction when the portfolio struggles, demonstrating that execution and integration matter as much as the raw savings amount.

The integrated plan assumes reasonable luck. Some people won't get it. Job loss, illness, divorce, market crashes, and the slow realization that the numbers aren't working can all disrupt retirement plans that seemed solid. Understanding what recovery looks like — and what safety nets exist for people whose plans have already failed — is the part of retirement planning that almost no book addresses honestly.

When It Doesn't Go According to Plan

The optimistic retirement planning scenarios assume steady employment until our chosen retirement age, reasonable investment returns, no major health crises, stable marriages, and controlled spending, but reality delivers job losses at 58, market crashes in year two of retirement, divorces at 62, medical emergencies requiring $80,000 in out-of-pocket costs, and the gradual realization at 72 that the money is running out faster than expected. Someone who retires with what seemed like adequate savings can find themselves at 75 with a depleted portfolio, mounting healthcare costs, and 15-20 more years to fund, facing choices between catastrophic options like moving in with adult children, returning to work in their mid-70s, or spending down to Medicaid qualification.

Portfolio depletion happens through combinations of bad luck and bad decisions rather than single catastrophic events, and someone who retires in 2007 with $800,000 watches it drop to $480,000 by early 2009, then withdraws $40,000 for living expenses bringing it to $440,000, and even after the market recovery finds themselves permanently behind where they would have been retiring two years later. The sequence of returns risk that seems theoretical in planning becomes brutally real when living through it, and the person who experiences negative returns in years one through three of retirement might never recover to their starting portfolio value even if they live another 25 years, because selling stocks at depressed prices to fund living expenses locks in losses that can't benefit from subsequent recovery.

The forced early retirement from job loss or health problems destroys plans built around working until 65 or 67, and someone laid off at 59 faces the worst possible combination of too young for Medicare, too old to find comparable employment, too many years before Social Security reaches maximum value, and immediate need to either pay for individual health insurance at $1,200-1,800 per month or go without coverage during the exact years when health problems start emerging. The plan to work until 67 and retire with $900,000 becomes retiring at 59 with $550,000 and eight years of living expenses plus healthcare costs before Medicare, potentially consuming $400,000 of the portfolio before reaching 65 and leaving only $150,000 to fund the remaining 20-30 years.

Medical bankruptcy affects hundreds of thousands of Americans annually including many who have insurance but face catastrophic costs from serious illness, and someone diagnosed with cancer at 64 might face $50,000-100,000 in out-of-pocket costs over two years of treatment between deductibles, coinsurance, out-of-network specialists, experimental treatments insurance won't cover, and lost income from inability to work. The retirement portfolio built over 40 years gets consumed by two years of medical bills, and someone who planned to retire at 65 with $700,000 finds themselves at 66 with $200,000 after medical expenses, fundamentally changing what's possible for the remaining retirement years.

Divorce after 50 splits accumulated retirement assets just when we're approaching the years when we need them most, and someone at 58 with $800,000 in joint retirement accounts sees $400,000 go to their ex-spouse, potentially losing employer health insurance if covered under spouse's plan, facing single rather than married tax brackets, and needing to fund housing on one income instead of two. The detailed retirement plan built around $800,000 supporting two people now involves $400,000 supporting one person who also needs to find individual health insurance for seven years until Medicare and might pay $15,000-20,000 more in annual taxes as a single filer compared to married filing jointly.

The gradual realization that money is running out happens slowly rather than suddenly, with someone noticing at 70 that their portfolio has declined from $600,000 at retirement to $450,000 despite modest spending, and projecting forward to see it hitting zero around age 82-85 if current patterns continue. The response depends on how much time remains before depletion, with someone at 70 projecting depletion at 85 having 15 years to adjust versus someone at 78 projecting depletion at 82 having only four years and much more limited options for generating income or reducing expenses.

Reducing spending when already living modestly creates genuine hardship rather than just inconvenience, and someone spending $45,000 annually who needs to cut to $35,000 faces eliminating things that matter like helping grandchildren with college, traveling to see distant family, maintaining a car that provides independence, or living in an area where they have friends and community connections. The easy cuts to dining out and entertainment disappeared years ago, and what remains are necessities that can't be reduced without major lifestyle degradation like moving to cheaper housing in an area where we know no one, eliminating the car and relying on others for transportation, or cutting back on medical care and prescriptions to save money.

Going back to work in our 70s provides income but faces age discrimination, physical limitations, and employment gaps that make finding work difficult, and someone who is 73 applying for retail or service jobs competes with younger workers who are perceived as more energetic, more tech-savvy, and more likely to stay in the position long-term. The jobs available to 70-somethings tend toward part-time seasonal work at $12-15 per hour, providing maybe $8,000-12,000 annually before taxes, which helps but doesn't fundamentally solve a situation where expenses exceed income by $20,000 per year and the portfolio is depleting.

Reverse mortgages convert home equity into cash flow without requiring monthly payments, and someone with a $300,000 house who is 70 might receive $150,000 as a lump sum or $1,000 per month for life, with the loan balance growing over time through accumulated interest and fees until the house is sold at death or when moving to long-term care. The costs are substantial with origination fees of $6,000-10,000, ongoing mortgage insurance premiums, higher interest rates than traditional mortgages, and the reality that the loan balance often grows to exceed the home's value over 15-20 years, leaving nothing for heirs and potentially creating situations where the borrower owes more than the home is worth.

The decision to use a reverse mortgage depends on whether we have heirs who expect to inherit the home, whether we plan to stay in the house until death, and whether alternative options exist like selling the home and moving to cheaper housing that would free up equity without the high costs of reverse mortgages. Someone with $400,000 in home equity who sells and moves to a $200,000 house in a cheaper area has $200,000 in liquid assets that can be invested to generate $8,000 per year at 4% withdrawal rate without paying reverse mortgage fees and interest, though this requires accepting the disruption and emotional cost of moving from a longtime home.

Moving in with adult children provides housing and potentially caregiving but creates dependence and family tension, and someone who moves into their daughter's home at 74 saves $15,000-20,000 annually in housing costs but loses independence, privacy, and potentially the relationship quality they had with their daughter before living together. The arrangement works well in some families where multiple generations genuinely enjoy living together and have adequate space and resources, but it fails in situations where the parent's presence creates stress on the adult child's marriage, limits their career flexibility, or where the parent feels like a burden rather than a valued family member.

The subsidized housing options for seniors include Section 8 vouchers, public housing, and HUD-subsidized senior apartments with rents based on income, typically charging 30% of monthly income up to fair market rent limits, and someone with $1,500 in monthly Social Security might pay $450 for an apartment that would cost $1,200 on the open market. Wait lists run 1-3 years in most areas and much longer in expensive cities, making this a option to pursue proactively rather than in crisis, and the housing quality varies enormously from well-maintained modern facilities to deteriorating buildings in dangerous neighborhoods with insufficient security.

Medicaid provides healthcare coverage for low-income individuals including elderly people who have spent down their assets, and qualifying requires income below roughly $1,700 per month and assets below $2,000 for individuals, meaning someone needs to be genuinely poor rather than just cash-flow constrained with substantial home equity or retirement accounts. The spend-down process to reach Medicaid eligibility involves depleting retirement accounts to pay for healthcare and living expenses until assets fall below the threshold, and while the primary residence and one vehicle are exempt from asset limits, other resources must be exhausted before qualifying.

Supplemental Security Income provides cash assistance of roughly $900 per month for elderly or disabled individuals with very low income and assets, and this federal program creates a floor below which income cannot fall for people who qualify. Someone with only $600 in Social Security because of sporadic work history might receive $300 in SSI to bring total income to $900, and combined with SNAP benefits for food and Medicaid for healthcare, this creates a basic subsistence level that prevents complete destitution but requires living in poverty according to any reasonable definition.

SNAP benefits formerly called food stamps provide $200-280 per month for food purchases for individuals meeting income and asset limits, and someone with $1,200 in monthly Social Security and $1,500 in countable assets might qualify for $250 monthly in SNAP that makes food costs manageable. The program requires recertification every 6-12 months with documentation of income and assets, and the benefits get loaded onto an EBT card that works like a debit card at grocery stores, allowing recipients to purchase food items but not prepared meals, alcohol, or non-food items.

Energy assistance programs help low-income households pay heating and cooling bills through LIHEAP grants that might provide $300-600 annually toward utility costs, and someone struggling to afford $200 monthly electric bills in summer or $250 monthly heating costs in winter gets partial relief that makes the difference between comfortable temperature and choosing between heat and food. These programs require annual applications and income verification, and the benefit amounts vary by state and funding levels that change yearly based on federal appropriations.

Senior centers provide free or low-cost meals, social activities, exercise classes, and connection to other services, and someone who is isolated and struggling financially can get a nutritious lunch five days per week plus social interaction that combats the depression and isolation that often accompany financial struggles in old age. Some centers offer transportation assistance, health screenings, benefits enrollment help, and referrals to other services, making them valuable hubs for accessing the complex network of programs available to low-income seniors.

Legal aid organizations provide free legal help to low-income elderly people facing eviction, benefit denials, consumer fraud, or estate planning, and someone who receives a denial of disability benefits or faces losing their apartment can get representation without paying attorney fees that would be unaffordable. These organizations are oversubscribed and have waiting lists, but they provide essential services that prevent vulnerable elderly people from being steamrolled by systems they don't understand or entities with more resources and sophistication.

Bankruptcy provides a legal process to discharge unsecured debts like credit cards and medical bills, and someone who accumulated $60,000 in credit card debt and $40,000 in medical bills can eliminate these obligations and start fresh, though they lose non-exempt assets in the process and face credit damage for 7-10 years. The homestead exemption protects some home equity from bankruptcy creditors, varying by state from complete protection to only $25,000-75,000, and retirement accounts in 401k plans and IRAs receive substantial protection, meaning someone can file bankruptcy and emerge with their home and retirement savings intact while eliminating credit card and medical debt.

The Chapter 7 versus Chapter 13 bankruptcy distinction matters for people with regular income, where Chapter 7 liquidates non-exempt assets to pay creditors and discharges remaining debts within 3-4 months, while Chapter 13 creates a 3-5 year repayment plan for people with enough income to pay some portion of debts over time. Someone with $2,000 monthly Social Security and $30,000 in credit card debt likely qualifies for Chapter 7 and walks away debt-free, while someone with $4,000 monthly income and the same debt might need Chapter 13 with a plan to pay $200 monthly for five years to creditors, discharging the remaining balance at completion.

The strategic default and foreclosure option applies to people whose homes are underwater or where continuing to pay the mortgage doesn't make financial sense, and someone who owes $250,000 on a house worth $180,000 while struggling to make $1,800 monthly payments might stop paying and live rent-free for 6-18 months during the foreclosure process, then move to cheaper rental housing at $1,000 per month. The credit damage is severe but less important for elderly people who won't be applying for mortgages or car loans, and the freed-up cash flow from not paying an underwater mortgage might be the difference between making ends meet and complete financial collapse.

Annuitizing remaining assets through immediate annuities converts a lump sum into guaranteed lifetime income, and someone with $150,000 remaining at age 75 might exchange it for $900 per month for life, creating certainty about income though giving up access to principal and leaving nothing for heirs if death comes early. The breakeven age might be 90-95 depending on the annuity terms and interest rates, meaning we need to live into our 90s to receive more than we paid in, but the value is the longevity insurance of knowing the income continues regardless of how long we live or what happens to investment markets.

The life insurance conversion option allows people with permanent life insurance policies to access the cash value through surrendering the policy for its cash surrender value or selling it through a life settlement to investors who pay more than surrender value but less than death benefit. Someone with a $100,000 whole life policy that has $30,000 cash surrender value might receive $40,000-50,000 from a life settlement company who then owns the policy and receives the death benefit when the insured dies, and this conversion of an illiquid asset into immediate cash can provide relief in a financial crisis though it eliminates the death benefit that would have gone to heirs.

The family loans and gifts from adult children provide assistance without the stigma of government programs, and someone whose children are financially successful might receive $1,000 per month in financial help that makes the difference between poverty and modest comfort. The challenge is that not all children are able or willing to provide support, and relationships can suffer when parents become financially dependent on children or when siblings disagree about who should contribute what amount to supporting parents, creating family conflict during already difficult times.

Downsizing possessions through selling furniture, jewelry, collections, and other accumulated items generates one-time cash while also reducing storage needs and simplifying life, and someone who sells $15,000 worth of furniture, an inherited jewelry collection, and their coin collection gets a temporary boost that buys time to implement longer-term solutions. The emotional difficulty of letting go of items with sentimental value or items that represented success and status during working years can be substantial, but the alternative of keeping things we can't afford to store or maintain while struggling financially makes less sense.

The roommate option for elderly people involves sharing housing costs with another senior who is also struggling financially, and someone paying $1,200 per month for a one-bedroom apartment might find another senior to split a $1,600 two-bedroom apartment, reducing costs to $800 each while also providing companionship and someone to check on them if health problems arise. The screening and compatibility challenges are real, and living with a stranger at 75 requires adjustment after decades of living alone or with only a spouse, but the financial and social benefits make this option worth considering for isolated seniors struggling with housing costs.

The gig economy and informal work opportunities include babysitting grandchildren for pay, helping neighbors with tasks like grocery shopping or lawn care, selling crafts online, or participating in medical research studies that pay participants, generating $200-500 monthly without formal employment that might be difficult to obtain. These options work better for healthier seniors in their late 60s and early 70s than for people in their 80s with mobility or cognitive limitations, and the income helps but rarely solves a fundamental shortfall between expenses and resources.

The acceptance that retirement as imagined isn't possible and adjustment to a different reality becomes necessary when all the numbers are run and the conclusion is that the money won't last without major changes. Someone who planned for travel and leisure might need to accept a retirement of part-time work and frugal living, and someone who hoped to leave an inheritance to children might need to use all their resources for their own survival, and these adjustments to expectations are painful but less painful than denial that leads to crisis when money runs out completely.

The lesson for people earlier in their financial journey is that the safety margin matters more than optimal returns, and someone who retires with $1,200,000 and 3% withdrawal rate has cushion to weather market crashes, medical emergencies, and unexpected expenses, while someone who retires with $600,000 and 6% withdrawal rate faces crisis from the same events. The extra years of work or reduced spending during accumulation years that build larger portfolio balances provide resilience that makes the difference between uncomfortable adjustments in retirement and genuine crisis, and planning conservatively with margin for error creates options that aggressive plans eliminate.

Don't miss out!

Visit the website below and you can sign up to receive emails whenever Matthew Thomas publishes a new book. There's no charge and no obligation.

https://books2read.com/r/B-A-ICCIF-MOUCJ

BOOKS 2 READ

Connecting independent readers to independent writers.

Did you love *Retire Without a Pension: Plan and Invest with 401k, IRA, and Social Security*? Then you should read *The Career Stall: Why You're Not Getting Promoted and How to Start Moving Again*[1] by Matthew Thomas!

[2]

Most career advice is written for people who are just starting out. It talks about working hard, building skills, and showing up. But somewhere around year five or ten, a lot of people do all of that and still stop moving. The reviews stay strong. The feedback stays vague. And the promotions go to someone else.

What actually happens at mid-career is different from what most career advice accounts for, and the frustration comes from applying the right advice to the wrong problem. Working harder does not fix a manager who is blocking you. Getting another certification does not fix an organization that almost never promotes from within. Being more visible does not fix a ceiling that has nothing to do with performance.

---

1. https://books2read.com/u/491jOW

2. https://books2read.com/u/491jOW

The Career Stall covers the full picture of why people get stuck: organizations that say they promote from within but almost never do, managers who are blocking advancement whether deliberately or not, skills gaps that have nothing to do with technical training, and ceilings that are invisible because no one will name them directly. It also covers what actually works: how to read whether your organization promotes, how to have the honest conversation about what it would take, when a lateral move is genuinely strategic and when it is just a delay, and how to job search while employed without tipping off your manager or burning the relationship on your way out.

The last chapter follows seven real people through their stalls: a software engineer stuck at senior level for six years, a marketing manager blocked by a territorial director, a healthcare administrator doing director-level work at manager pay, a professional who spent three years and $85,000 on an MBA that did not solve the problem because the problem was never the credential, a sales manager who realized he was happier and better paid as an individual contributor, an analyst who got promoted after changing how she communicated but was conflicted about whether the change should have been necessary, and an HR manager who stayed too long at a declining company and got laid off before he left on his own terms.

Every one of them eventually got unstuck. None of them did it by being more patient or working harder at their current level. They did it by figuring out what was actually blocking them and acting on that specifically, rather than continuing to optimize for the stated problem while the real one stayed fixed.

If you have been at the same level for more than two years and cannot get a clear answer about what it would take to move forward, this is for you.Approximately 35,000 words.

www.ingramcontent.com/pod-product-compliance
Lightning Source LLC
LaVergne TN
LVHW100308210926
848480LV00003B/1062
9798233893339